The Jacobite Rising of 1715 and the Murray Family

To my mother,
Janice Norma Peace,
who initiated my love of history
and rescued it in 1985.

The Jacobite Rising of 1715 and the Murray Family

Brothers in Arms

Rosalind Anderson

PEN & SWORD
HISTORY

First published in Great Britain in 2020 by
Pen & Sword History
An imprint of
Pen & Sword Books Ltd
Yorkshire – Philadelphia

ISBN 978 1 52672 761 9

A CIP catalogue record for this book is
available from the British Library.

Printed and bound in the UK by TJ International Ltd,
Padstow, Cornwall.

Pen & Sword Books Limited incorporates the imprints of Atlas,
Archaeology, Aviation, Discovery, Family History, Fiction, History,
Maritime, Military, Military Classics, Politics, Select, Transport,
True Crime, Air World, Frontline Publishing, Leo Cooper, Remember
When, Seaforth Publishing, The Praetorian Press, Wharncliffe
Local History, Wharncliffe Transport, Wharncliffe True Crime
and White Owl.

For a complete list of Pen & Sword titles please contact

PEN & SWORD BOOKS LIMITED
47 Church Street, Barnsley, South Yorkshire, S70 2AS, England
E-mail: enquiries@pen-and-sword.co.uk
Website: www.pen-and-sword.co.uk

Or

PEN AND SWORD BOOKS
1950 Lawrence Rd, Havertown, PA 19083, USA
E-mail: Uspen-and-sword@casematepublishers.com
Website: www.penandswordbooks.com

Contents

List of Illustrations

Murray Family Tree

JOHN
MARQUIS
OF ATHOLL
1631 – 1703
Married
AMELIA
MARCHIONESS
OF ATHOLL
1633 – 1703

JOHN MURRAY
1660-1724
EARL OF TULLIBARDINE
1696-1703
2ND MARQUIS OF ATHOLL 1703
DUKE OF ATHOLL 1703

Married
KATHERINE HAMILTON
1662-1707
COUNTESS OF TULLIBARDINE
1696-1703
DUCHESS OF ATHOLL 1703

CHARLES 1661-1710
EARL OF DUNMORE 1686

CHARLOTTE 1662-1735

JAMES 1663-1719

WILLIAM 1664-1726
LORD NAIRNE 1690
Married MARGARET NAIRNE

AMELIA 1666-1743
LADY LOVAT 1685
DOWAGER LOVAT 1696

MUNGO 1668-1700

EDWARD 1669-1767

HENRY 1670

KATHERINE 1572-1686

GEORGE 1673 -1691

JOHN (Johny)
1684 – 1709
MARQUIS OF TULLIBARDINE
1703 – 1709

ANNE 1685 – 1686

MARY 1686 – 1689

AMELIA 1687-1689

WILLIAM 1689 – 1746
MARQUIS OF TULLIBARDINE
1709 – 1746

JAMES 1690 – 1764
2ND DUKE OF ATHOLL 1724 – 1764

CHARLES 1691 – 1720

KATHERINE 1692 – 1692

GEORGE 1693 – 1693

GEORGE 1694 – 1760

SUSAN 1699 – 1725

KATHERINE 1702 – 1710

BASIL 1704 – 1712

Hamilton Family Tree

ANNE

3rd DUCHESS

OF HAMILTON

1632 – 1716

Married

WILLIAM

EARL OF SELKIRK

AND 3rd DUKE

OF HAMILTON

1634-1694

MARY 1657-1666

JAMES 1658 – 1712

EARL OF ARRAN

4th DUKE OF HAMILTON

WILLIAM 1659 – 1681

ANNA 1661 – 1663

KATHERINE 1662 – 1707

COUNTESS OF TULLIBARDINE

1696-1703

DUCHESS OF ATHOLL 1703

CHARLES 1664 – 1739

EARL OF SELKIRK

JOHN 1665 – 1744

EARL OF RUGLEN

GEORGE 1666 – 1737

EARL OF ORKNEY

SUSAN 1667 – 1737

MARGARET 1668 – 1731

COUNTESS OF PANMURE

ANNA 1669-1669

BASIL 1671 – 1701

ARCHIBALD 1673 – 1754

Acknowledgements

This book would never have materialised without the help of a group of patient and reliable friends, colleagues and new acquaintances. Initially it was Fiona Davidson, Learning Services Officer at Historic Environment Scotland, who saw a fresh angle in my proposal for an education tour at Huntingtower Castle, without her support the idea would never have got off the ground. I owe a significant debt of gratitude to Keren Guthrie at the Blair Archives who was generous with her time and efforts as well as her knowledge on the Murray family. I am very grateful to Blair Castle for allowing me access to their archives and to reproduce images from their collection. In addition I would like to thank the Hamilton Archives for permission to access and use their letters. Assistance given by Jo Dixon at the National Register of Archives for Scotland was very much appreciated as was the knowledge and information from Nicola Cowmeadow at the A.K. Library in Perth on both Katherine Hamilton and Margaret Nairne. Once the book proposal was accepted, for which I thank Pen and Sword, my times of weakness were assisted by Joanne Safe who has faithfully stuck by me whatever my choices in life; Laura Gilmartin, who patiently listens to my ramblings; Freda Jenkins, who read the initial draft chapters and responded so positively, and most of all to Sarah Anderson, who read the whole manuscript, corrected, questioned and harassed me into getting it finished. Thanks also to the helpful people at the Dunblane Museum and to Sam Hardie for assisting with the images in my hour of need! My family too deserve my gratitude, especially Cameron and Jennifer Anderson for putting up with having this book in their lives, always supporting me and having such a positive conviction that I could complete it.

Introduction

Perthshire, August 1715. After a tense week, two brothers set off from their family home of Blair Castle, to go to their grandmother's house in Hamilton. They carried a letter from their father which stated it should be burned after being read. It described the heated discussions and emotions of the previous week at Blair and, not for the first time, asked for the grandmother's help to smooth relations between father and eldest son. The second son was to join another brother, already at her home, and go on to their military posts in Ireland. But the brothers never made it to Hamilton and Dowager Duchess Anne (the grandmother) never received the letter. Instead the brothers headed to another property of their father's in Perthshire where they wrote to a cousin, one of the Nairnes, a family well known for its Jacobite sympathies. They then headed north to the Braes of Mar where, with other leading lords and clan chiefs, they joined the Earl of Mar and so began the Great Rising of 1715.

The Duke of Atholl, the father, was genuinely surprised by the involvement of his sons William, Charles and George in the rising. In fact, for a while he was still under the impression it was only William who was involved, but he learned the truth later and on 13 February 1716, in a letter to his mother-in-law, Dowager Duchess Anne Hamilton, he wrote, 'what grieved me most is that the children of so excellent a mother should have been capable of such a thing.'[1]

The previous decades had seen dramatic change in Scotland. Five monarchies in thirty years with the associated changes of governments, along with the Treaty of Union in 1707, had radically altered what was, in effect, was a power vacuum in Scotland, left by an absentee monarch since the Union of the Crowns. With the death of Queen Anne's heir at the start of the new century, the future was uncertain and no landowning family or clan in Scotland could comfortably feel secure in its power base. The new centre of power in London was attracting growing numbers of Scottish nobles south, but as England was almost permanently involved in a European war, affairs in Scotland were increasingly being dragged into a wider political mix, with foreign powers willing to use it as a tool for their own ends. External influences, both economical and political, were playing more and more of a role in shaping the future of the country. What had previously been a country on the periphery was now integral to the world stage. A proud nation with a strong feeling of tradition, there were many in Scotland who still felt a strong loyal allegiance to the Stuarts, the royal family which had ruled the country since Robert II, the son of Robert the Bruce's daughter Marjory and Walter Stewart, the Lord High Steward of Scotland. But it was comparatively a very poor country, with a small population and inefficient means of communication, all of which were to play a major role in events in the 1690s and the lead up to the Rising of 1715.

As any parent discovers, in any age, guaranteeing the loyalty and cooperation of independent-minded children each with their own character and sense of purpose is very difficult. Controlling the lives of five sons during this time of turmoil was, for Atholl, impossible. The duke himself had to be pragmatic and traditionally is seen as having latent Jacobite sympathies, hedging his bets during this rising as in the Ballad of Sheriffmuir:

> Brave gen'rous Southesk, Tullibardine was brisk,
> Whose father indeed would not draw, man,
> Into the same yoke, which serv'd for a cloak,
> To keep the estate 'twixt them twa, man.[2]

However, a look at the earlier years of the family through letters, incidents and influences during this time sheds a very different light as it becomes clear that four of his sons possessed a strong rebellious streak. Despite the heavily enforced regime in their childhood of responsibility and duty from their father and the Presbyterian piety of their mother, these brothers refused to conform to their parents' wishes and in varying degrees chose, of their own volition, a different path to that expected of them. These choices had a significant impact on the history of the family and, because of who that family was, also a significant impact on the country.

The majority of the evidence for this work has been taken from contemporary letters written by the main protagonists and their relations. These letters are a superb primary source material as they shine a light on not only the main political and social events of the time but more particularly, in this case, on the colour and detail that gets lost in a factual historical narrative. Reading a handwritten letter is a very different experience to reading one written in Times New Roman Font in a book or on a computer screen. The feelings, emotion and intensity get lost in print, while handling an original document where individual writing can be recognised, and changes observed indicating perhaps speed, stress or distress is emotive and gives a strong sense of the story being about real, fallible people.

Nevertheless, it is important to remember that the letters read are the ones that survive, and thus don't give us the whole picture. In fact, in many cases they raise more questions that can't be answered, and frustratingly crucial gaps appear. Many letters are missing, some were lost at the time, the correspondents complain of not having received replies, some maybe don't even exist, i.e. an answer wasn't given, but many were intentionally destroyed, and they were probably the more interesting. Significantly, after the death of the Duchess of Atholl, there is also a distinct change in quantity and content in the Murray family letters, which means we are deprived of what would have given us a fuller picture of family life in the crucial years. However, a compelling picture can still be constructed of what was happening in the Murray household and how this would have affected any children and teenagers, as the brothers were, growing up in it.

To fully appreciate the twists and turns of the family life, it is necessary first to put it into the context of what Scotland was experiencing at this time, as the decade at the end of the seventeenth century witnessed several significant and pivotal events which are still debated today.

Chapter 1

Scotland in the Seventeenth Century

The seventeenth century in Scotland ended with a decade of major political, social and economic drama, the impact of which was to have far reaching consequences for decades, if not centuries to come. It began with the Massacre of Glencoe in 1692, one of the most atrocious acts perpetrated on British soil, and ended with the economic disaster of the Darien scheme which effectively bankrupted the country. The intervening 'ill' years were dominated by famine and disease during which, for the last time, the majority of the country's population faced the threat of starvation. For many, the target for blame was directed south, to the new monarch, King William. He showed no interest in his kingdom north of the border, other than as a possible source of men for his army, obsessed as he was with fighting Catholic France.

William of Orange and his wife Mary, the daughter of James VII of Scotland and II of England, had come to the throne through the Glorious Revolution in 1688. They were invited by both Tory and Whig MPs in England who were alarmed at the strategy and government of the current monarch, James VII & II, and more significantly, the birth of a son to his second wife, the Catholic Mary of Modena. William, a Protestant Dutch Stahdholder, accepted the invitation and arrived as a conquering hero to save the nation from Catholicism. With little resistance in England, his main opposition was in Ireland and Scotland where Jacobites, (from the Latin for James, Jacobus) continued to support the Stuart King James.

James VII & II had hoped he could defend his crown from Ireland, but was defeated at the Battle of the Boyne in 1690 and fled to France never to return. In Scotland it was John Graham Claverhouse, Viscount of Dundee, who raised the standard for James and with some success, due to his personal leadership. But he didn't have universal support and although he led a Highland force which defeated the Williamites at the Battle of Killiecrankie in 1689, he was fatally injured and the Jacobites were then defeated at the Battle of Dunkeld, and later at the Battle of Cromdale. News of the Irish defeat and James' exile to France dampened any enthusiasm for supporting the Stuart king, but suspicion from the south of Jacobite intentions continued. The new government's perception of its northern region was of militarily minded Catholic Highlanders, seething with resentment, who were willing to take any opportunity to rebel.

In an attempt to enforce authority on the Highland Chiefs and extinguish any remnant support for James, a pardon for all clans was offered as long as an oath of allegiance was taken before a magistrate by 1 January 1692. After seeking the agreement of James VII in France, which he granted, although news of this was delayed and didn't arrive till late December 1691, nearly all chiefs agreed, including the aged McIain of Glencoe, chief of a small branch of the MacDonald Clan. However, McIain left it late and went to the wrong person, as Colonel Hill at Inverlochy wasn't empowered to administer the oath. After an arduous journey though hard winter weather the 70-year-old chief eventually arrived at Inverary too late, as the Sheriff, Campbell of Arkinglas, was on holiday for New Year. When news reached Edinburgh of the lateness, the Secretary of State John Dalrymple, a Protestant lowlander, decided to make an example of the clan. He issued the order which was carried out by Robert Campbell of Glenlyon, in command of a company in the Earl of Argyll's Regiment of Foot:

> You are hereby ordered to fall upon the rebels, the MacDonalds of Glencoe, and put all to the sword under seventy. You are to have special care the the Old Fox and his sons doe upon no account escape your hands, you are to secure all the avenues that no man escape … . This is by the King's special command for the good and safety of the country that these miscreants be cutt of root and branch.[1]

The soldiers, under Campbell, had arrived at Glencoe twelve days earlier, claiming the garrison at Fort William was full, and had been offered the traditional Highland hospitality by the clan. After days of eating, drinking, sleeping and entertaining with their hosts, on the snowy morning of 13 February, the soldiers eventually received their orders and set about killing. It seems likely some of the soldiers warned members of the clan and allowed them to escape, but thirty-eight people were slaughtered in their homes – including the chief, MacIain.

News of the massacre was met with widespread shock and horror, and due to political and public anger in 1696 the Scottish Parliament ordered a full inquiry. But of course King William, who had signed the order, could not be seen to be responsible so the result was a predictable cover up. Over-zealous soldiers were blamed and though Dalrymple lost his job as Secretary of State, within a few years he was created Earl of Stair by Queen Anne and was involved in the negotiations for the Act of Union in 1707. Despite the inquiry and its findings, there was a strong and lasting perception that the Act had been an extreme incident in the clan rivalry of the Campbells and MacDonalds and it increased the hatred felt by many towards the dominating, government-supporting, Protestant Campbells. This continued existence of ancient clan rivalries in many parts of Scotland was not unique and would reappear throughout the Jacobite rebellions.

Since the union of the crowns in 1603 when James VI of Scotland added to his title that of James I of England, Scotland had been forced to function under an absentee monarch. In the vacuum left by a royal court, clan chiefs and leading nobles were able to increase their strength and influence in the country while secretaries of state handled everything on behalf of the king. Almost inevitably, rivalries would fester and grow as each magnate sought dominance over the other. The scene was dominated by a few leading nobles including the Duke of Queensberry, Duke of Hamilton, Marquis of Atholl and the Duke of Argyll, many of whom would play significant roles in the lives of the Murray brothers as well as the destiny of the country. Clan chiefs still dominated in the Highlands, but not to the extent they had in the previous century when, on a word, a Highland Chief could call on a large number of retainers and kin to follow him to war, in return for which tenants and kin were given protection and sustenance. By the 1650s this social custom was non-existent in the Lowlands, but it continued in varying forms in the Highlands where tradition remained strong.

All landowners relied heavily on rent from tenants, but frequently this was in kind rather than coinage, so that they were directly affected by the success or otherwise of the heavily rural economy. Lack of coinage in the economy meant a poorer standard of living in the country as a whole, compared to their southern counterparts and keeping up with the lifestyle of Westminster Lords was not an ambition many of the Scottish nobility could contemplate. Many were reluctant to travel to London at all. The distances were great, the roads uncomfortable as well as dangerous, and the cost of travelling and lodging was a huge burden. Writing in 1689, Rev. Thomas Morer, an army chaplain to a Scottish regiment fighting for William of Orange, gave a descriptive image of the situation:

> Stage coaches they have none yet there are a few hackneys in Edinburg [*sic*], which they may hire into the country upon urgent occasions. The truth is the roads will hardly allow 'em the conveniences, which is the reason that their gentry, men and women, chuse rather to use their horses. However their great men often travel with coach and six, but with so much caution, that besides their other attendance, they have a lusty running footman on each side the coach to manage and keep it in rough places.[2]

Descriptions of this nature are common among the few travellers from England who ventured north, with the majority feeding a general negative image of the country and people. Until General Wade initiated the construction of a network of roads across the Highlands in 1725, north of Stirling and Edinburgh there were no roads as such, just tracks, which were almost impassable for a four-wheeled cart – even in good weather. However, half of the total population of approximately 1 million lived north of the Tay, and a significant amount lived in the Highlands, a far higher percentage than today. The economy was overwhelmingly rural and, for the majority, at subsistence level. There was some grain trade, with surplus being sent to the towns and areas where more tenants were involved in rearing cattle, sheep and goats. But in general, the infield-outfield farming system (infield being the more fertile land and outfield the poorer) which was practised in most areas of the country was inefficient and didn't allow for any development or innovation. The main crops were oats and barley, which, when impacted by consecutive seasons of bad weather, resulted fairly quickly in severe hardship and on occasion famine. The years of the 1690s were particularly bad and, if not actually the worst, were the last time people died of hunger in such large numbers.

The 'Ill years' as they became known, began in 1695 with a particularly bad harvest so that by 1696 the fiar prices, (when the price of grain was fixed in the county) had reached heights unparalleled for decades. As autumn progressed, wet weather continued and though there was slight relief in 1697, the worst harvests were to occur in 1698 when the country was experiencing extreme weather including snow in May, followed by months of drought in summer and cyclones in autumn. In addition many areas were hit by disease, most notably typhus and smallpox. All sections of society were affected by this and it was to have repercussions for some time, with population numbers not recovering to previous levels for many years. The Scottish physician Sir Robert Sibbald, wrote in 1699: 'Everyone may see death in the face of the poor that almost everywhere the thinness of their visage, the ghostly looks, their feebleness, the agues and their fluxes threaten them with sudden death'. On 4 March 1697, the Earl of Marchmont wrote to the Earl of Tullibardine:

> As the last year had been one of the worst and most unfruitful that had been seen by any now living, so it had a very bad influence upon every fund of the revenue and public payments. The cess came never worse in; and the excise so ill as that it has never failed beyond expectation. None have more reason to be sensible of this than the Lords of the Treasury.[3]

The writer and politician Andrew Fletcher of Saltoun began his *Second Discourse Concerning The Affairs of Scotland*, in 1698 with: 'The first thing I humbly and earnestly propose to that honourable court is that they would take into their consideration the condition of so many thousands of our people who are at this day dying for want of bread.'

Fletcher was a supporter of the Darien scheme, an attempt by the Scottish elite to break the ties of dependence on agriculture and copy the success of the English East India company, by setting up a trading company in the west. William Paterson, one of the founding directors of the Bank of England, hit on the idea of the Isthmus of Panama being the gateway to global trade linking Europe with the America's, China and India. Investors throughout Scotland from all sections of society, but particularly the majority of the wealthiest families, were persuaded that this was the break the country needed and in a short time managed to raise £400,000, a considerable amount given the poor state of the country's economy and estimated to be half the total capital. It began with great enthusiasm and optimism, with many leading family members encouraging others to invest in what was seen as a great opportunity.

In 1695 royal assent was granted to the Act which established a Company of Scotland Trading to Africa, and three ships were ordered from Hamburgh and Amsterdam, to transport the colonists and trade goods. The first expedition set sail from Leith on 12 July 1698 and arrived in November, with the settlers taking possession of a narrow promontory they called Caledonia. It wasn't long before reality hit, however, and the colonists were suffering from tropical disease, starvation and internal feuds. The area was surrounded by land occupied by the Spanish who were none too keen on a rival in the area and mobilised against them. Despite the initial royal approval, King William quickly withdrew his support to appease the East India Company whose monopoly was threatened by the Scots Company, but also as he didn't want to offend Spain while he was pursuing his war against France. Dutch and English merchants were therefore forbidden to trade with the Scots and the promised English investment was stopped.

A supply ship sent in January 1699 was shipwrecked and the second expedition, unaware of the disasters affecting the first colonists, was itself hit by disaster with around 160 dying on the voyage out. The ship had been refused water and food by the governor at Montserrat, acting under instructions received from England that the Darien Colony was illegal. When the expedition finally arrived in August 1700, it found the colony abandoned so its crew set about trying to rebuild huts while they waited for the lead ship, the *Rising Sun*, to arrive. However, one of the men dropped a candle among the liquor on the provision ship which set fire and destroyed all the stores.

Despite these disasters the Scots managed to pull off a brilliant attack against Spanish forces at Toubacanti, but it was a short-lived victory, as a massive fleet of Spanish ships arrived in March 1700 under the command of Governor General Pimiento. The colonists surrendered and after signing a capitulation in the rain, were allowed to leave on board their remaining ships while a piper played. However, their trials didn't stop there, one of the returning ships was wrecked in Jamaica and another declared unfit to sail; during the return voyage fever broke out again and the *Rising Sun* was lost off Charleston with around 140 colonists. Reports at the time said that only thirty people returned to Scotland.

The disaster was demoralising and embarrassing and had a direct influence on the negotiations for the Act of Union 1707, many being persuaded that economically, on its own, Scotland could not compete as it desperately needed access to growing trade routes. As part of the Union agreement England paid a sum of £398,000, most of which went to cover the Company of Scotland's losses, and it was to this that Robert Burns famously referred in *Such a Parcel of Rogues in a Nation*:

> But pith and power, till my last hour,
> I'll mak this declaration;
> We're bought and sold for English gold–
> Such a parcel of rogues in a nation!

This, then, was the decade in which the Murray brothers grew up and formed the background to their adulthood. The family, because of who they were and their position in society, were directly affected by these events. Prominent family members were significantly involved in all of the events, and this inevitably must have had an impact on the minds and opinions of the brothers.

Chapter 2

John Murray, Earl of Tullibardine

The Atholl Murrays were among the elite of Scottish nobility. Their lands stretched from Dunkeld, in the heart of Perthshire to the borders of Inverness-shire and included Lowland properties of Tullibardine, Huntingtower, Falkland and a town house in Perth, as well as lands in Balquhidder. It was a regality ruled by a succession of families and for most of its history that ownership had in fact been the Stewarts. The main property was Blair Castle near Pitlochry and this central position was essential for forces travelling north or south. The Murray's ownership began in the seventeenth century with John Murray, the Earl of Tullibardine, being created Earl of Atholl in the peerage of 1629. By 1706 the Duke of Atholl could claim to be able to call out between 3–4000 fencible men,[1] a significant number, matched by few other landowners or clan chiefs. Murray support was therefore sought by both sides during the rebellions in the knowledge it could make a crucial difference.

Lord John Murray, the future first duke, was the eldest son of the Marquis of Atholl and his wife Lady Amelia Sophia Stanley, third daughter of James 7th Earl of Derby. The contemporary politician and Jacobite, George Lockhart of Carnwath, described Murray as:

> ... endowed with good natural parts, though by reason of his proud, imperious, haughty, passionate temper he was no ways capable to be the leading man of a party which he aimed at ... He was reputed very brave, but hot and headstrong and tho' no scholar nor orator, yet express'd his mind very handsomely on publick occasions.[2]

John Macky, in his memoirs of the times wrote 'He is of a very proud, fiery, partial disposition; does not want sense, but choaks himself with passion, which is easily would up when he speaks in public assemblies.'[3] A painting currently at Blair Castle is a good representation of these descriptions. It used to hang at Huntingtower, where in 1711 his brother Lord Nairne commented: 'I thought my dear brother look'd very gracefully in yr robes at Huntingtower but to be sure the collar of the Thistle & being so near the Queen wd add not a little to yr good mein.'[4]

Throughout his life, and in comparison to the later dukes, it is evident that John Murray's sense of duty and responsibility to his tenants, as well as loyalty to his family, was genuine and sincere. As the head of the Atholl estates his area of authority was vast. Unlike traditional Highland estates the Atholl lands, which consisted of highland and lowlands areas, was a regality, a territorial jurisdiction governed more by land ownership than traditional blood ties. As duke, for example, he had the power of life and death in the regality courts, and appointments to the much sought-after military posts were entirely dependent on his goodwill. Later dukes were to become more preoccupied with London politics and land management, but John Murray represented more of the old-style magnate, attentively involved and committed to local affairs and the welfare of his tenants. This approach was apparent in his involvement in helping introduce formal education in the Highlands. He was a founder member of the Society for Propagating Christian Knowledge (SSPCK) founded in 1709 and based in Edinburgh. Its mission was to establish and manage schools in the Highland and Islands, to secure both the 1690 Presbyterian settlement of the Church of Scotland and the 1707 Act of Union. With the duke's support (despite his being notoriously anti-union) the society set up one of the earliest schools in Blair Atholl, and not long after, in Balquhidder. The schoolmaster James Murray wrote in 1716, 'that his grace the Duke of Atholl is most kind to him ... and that his grace has been pleased to write to all his vassals tenants and people to countenance his school and send their children to it.'[5]

The SSPCK was criticised heavily for its insistence on the use of the English language only. It believed that by spreading English literacy, the Highlands would be won over to the political and religious establishment of the government and its people would then become loyal subjects. However, in many cases, as the schoolmasters frequently spoke no Gaelic, pupils were just repeating texts by rote, without understanding what they were saying. Despite the society's insistence on the use of English, however, there is evidence the duke was enlightened enough to realise this was impractical and was an issue he didn't agree with. He was determined, for example, that his eldest son and heir Johny was able to speak Gaelic. In 1699 Johny was sent by his father to the 'highlands to lairne Irish',[6] and a description of one of the rooms at Huntingtower in 1696 mentions the fact there were Irish bibles there for his tenants (by Irish it meant Gaelic). Also, in 1718 the duke replied to the Fortingall presbytery 'that Mr Campbell was not so fit to be sent to Fortingall not having the Irish language',[7] and therefore unable to preach to the local people there.

His moral obligation to help promote education came from his concern for the spiritual welfare of his people and in this he was strongly supported by his wife. Murray married Lady Katherine Hamilton in 1683 with the agreed jointure property being Huntingtower.[8] In 1684 he wrote to his father-in-law the Duke of Hamilton, asking for money to be spent on Huntingtower, instead of Falkland[9] where they were living, as he intended to spend more time there and needed to accommodate his ever expanding family. The Murrays made major changes to Huntingtower which, after these renovations, would have been an impressive building and far more extensive than what remains today. The two towers were formally joined in stone, more rooms were added as well as a staircase, and more substantial outbuildings were developed. Murray claimed he was unprepared for running his own home and later explained to his son William: 'I found myself at a loss when I was first married having never been anyways concerned in country affairs before and then having taken up a separate house from my father, I had no means or opportunity to be acquainted with the method of managing country business.'[10]

Murray had converted to the Presbyterian church shortly before his marriage; whether this was of pragmatic necessity after the arrival of King William, part of the agreement for his marriage, or from genuine religious belief is hard to tell, though his commitment to his new faith can't be faulted. That he was religious and probably more pious than most is evident in his letters and religious observance, but he was clearly not as strict as his wife. For a long time his attitude was fairly tolerant – his parents, after all, remained Episcopalian; however, he wasn't prepared to tolerate any 'popish' practices. In a letter to his second son in 1707 he explained his views:

> But beside this it is and has been my own opinion since I was 18yrs of age and I learned it during my travels in France where I happened to stay for some months at Angers in a Protestant ministers house called Mr Lombard, where I first had occasion to observe that these were good Protestants without being Episcopals, and some thousands of ministers of that nation with millions of Protestants that lived then in France have shown themselves by their sufferings and persecutions they have endured on account of their Religion, that they were good Protestants. And then it was that I began to understand the unreasonableness to make a difference as to Protestants that did not differ in essentials.[11]

The religious settlement of 1690 had established the Church of Scotland as Presbyterian and had abolished patronage. Instead, ministers were appointed by church elders and heritors in the parish, although magnates like the Atholls still had considerable influence. Katherine repeatedly urged her husband to use this power to secure the posts for Presbyterians, but as this frequently led to resistance, on most occasions Murray was satisfied to accept an Episcopalian in the post as long as they followed the law and agreed to pray for King William and Queen Mary. After Queen Anne's accession he maintained this stance; for example, in 1706 he supported the case of Episcopal ministers in Perthshire, asking the Earl of Mar to lay the case before the queen as he regarded them as being good and peaceable men.

However, his tolerant attitude was to change when the threat of rebellion began in 1715. A large percentage of Jacobite rebels were Episcopalian, and Murray needed to distance himself as much as possible from them. Despite a reputation for hedging his bets to ensure the estate stayed in the hands of the family, it is unlikely that in 1715 the then duke seriously entertained a notion of aligning himself with the Jacobites, no matter how much they offered him to join them. His refusal was not because he didn't have any sympathy with their cause as he himself was anti-union, but came down to the fact that James was a Roman Catholic:

> I learned another thing when in France which was to dislike the popish religion more than formerly, for I could not have believed that their principles and practice were so gross as I found them there and if ever these nations have the misfortune to have a popish king you will find that a popish head is inconsistent with a Protestant body and people.[12]

Initially, however, Lord Murray's political career had benefited from his being associated with both Episcopalian and Presbyterianism.

In December 1688 Murray had been one of the first wave of nobility to go down to London to greet William, and continued to show himself loyal to the new king during the 1689 rebellion, by refusing to join Bonnie Dundee at Killiecrankie. Despite repeated requests by Dundee that Murray hold Blair Castle for King James, he ignored him and instead urged the Atholl men to be loyal to the government. Unfortunately his plea met with little success as many fought with Dundee and later joined the rebels under the command of Murray's brother, Lord James, for which John Murray was severely censured by the government troops leader General Mackay:

> ... your lordship gave me much assurance they would not joyn Dundie as long as you were in the countrey, notwithstanding that, I know your brother, whom I saw you with that morning, to be actually present with that party with the greater parte of the Athollmen so that my Lord, I can say litle or nothing to your Lordship vindication ...'[13]

Murray's father had also been conveniently absent during the episode, excusing himself by claiming he had had to go to the baths due to his ill health which inevitably cast doubt on the family commitment. The marquis' loyalties to the crown were considered suspect anyway due to his Stuart Royalist past and the fact he and his wife were Episcopalian. Perhaps pragmatically then, to secure a profitable future for the family and estate it was necessary that Lord Murray's role be to represent the Williamite arm of the Atholl interest.

Despite a lacklustre performance at Killiecrankie, Murray gained some credit from the government for the stance he took, but he didn't gain any benefit for this until his appointment in 1693 as one of the commissioners on the inquiry into the Glencoe massacre. In a letter to his mother Murray detailed the measures he had taken to uncover the truth of this tragedy and wrote:

> ... it concerns the whole nation to have that barbarous action fully and clearly made out, and laied on the true author and contriver of itt, whoever itt be, and innocent blood is a crying sin, which all have reason to endeavour to bring the authors of it to light.[14]

Ultimately it was the then Secretary of State, John Dalrymple, who was found to have exceeded his orders and was dismissed from his post in 1695. He was replaced by Lord Murray in 1696 who shared the post with Sir James Ogilvy, Lord Seafield. It could well be that Murray was chosen by William to be one of the Secretaries of State for Scotland because he uniquely bridged the divide between his Presbyterian and Episcopalian ministers. Others were less convinced of Murray's religious sincerity however, the Earl of Argyll writing to William Carstares in 1698 said: 'I think you ave better security for his Grace than any is yet got of our two year old Presbyterian the Marquis of Atholl's son the Earl of Tullibardine.'[15] But then there was no love lost between these two families, this earl's father, Archibald Campbell the 9th Earl of Argyll, had led a rebellion in 1685 which was put down by forces led by Murray's father, the Marquis of Atholl, and had ultimately ended with in Argyll's execution.

In 1696 Murray was made commissioner to the parliament; as only a peer could represent the king, he had to be raised to the peerage in his own right and was created Earl of Tullibardine. However, this period wasn't an easy one for him as his appointment was resented by the new 2nd Duke of Queensberry and the Earl of Argyll. Tullibardine worked tirelessly to build up support to match these rivals and to some extent was successful, despite also gaining a not too flattering reputation for claiming credit for any ministerial achievements advancing his own interest. The Earl of Seafield wrote: 'I am sure he has this year thrice as much from the King as I have got: He will improve all these favours for establishing his own power.'[16] But when he backed Sir William Hamilton of Whitelaw for President of the Court of Session he was left humiliated when the king appointed Hugh Dalrymple instead. Known widely as Whitelaw's sponsor and too proud to back down, Tullibardine resigned his post. He wrote to his father:

> This is to acquaint my dear father that I have this day resigned my place as Secretary to the King. The occasion of it is, that the King signed a commission for the Lord Whitelaw to be president of the Session before the last Parl which I carried down and promised in the King's name … the king nevertheless delayed it and has given it to another. I did not think my word and honour so much engaged in this that I cou'd not but show the world that it was not my fault that I have not performed my promise.[17]

Tullibardine's reaction to this perceived slight was fairly typical of his character. In addition to a determined sense of duty, responsibility and traditional paternalism, there was also a proud, imperious nature which, when crossed, led to outbursts of temper and arrogance. Several incidents in his lifetime demonstrated this particular trait in varying degrees among which were his threatening Lord Breadalbane to a duel,[18] and defending himself against five 'rogues' in Balquhidder by taking a shot at one of them.[19] The most public and vitriolic affair, however, was his conflict with Simon Fraser 11th Lord Lovat, known more famously as the Fox. After Tullibardine resigned his office as Secretary of State he returned to Scotland and the maelstrom of this particular saga which was dominating not only Murray family life but the majority of Scottish society.

Chapter 3

Murray and Fraser: An Ill-Fated Feud

John Murray and Simon Fraser's mutual abhorrence of each other played a significant role in Murray family life from the early 1690s and continued throughout John Murray's lifetime. It led to several crucial incidents which had lasting implications not only for the individuals themselves, but also their relations and followers. As it dominated the childhood and adolescence of the Murray brothers, it inevitably played a role in their opinions and future decision making.

Its origin was in 1685, with the marriage of Hugh 9th Lord Lovat and Chief of the Clan Fraser, to Amelia Murray, the marquis of Atholl's daughter and John Murray's sister. The contract was negotiated by the lawyer George Mackenzie of Tarbet (whose sister had been married to the 8th Lord Lovat) who saw it as a chance to increase his influence in the area, MacKenzie and Fraser lands being adjacent to each other, while the Murrays saw it as an opportunity to strengthen their ties in the Highlands.

The terms of the marriage, however, stated that on the death of the current Lord Lovat, the estate would pass to a daughter, if there were no sons, as long as she married a man of the name of Fraser. This effectively attempted to keep the inheritance in the Murray sphere of influence, while eliminating cadet branches of the clan from the Fraser hierarchy, but was not popular among the clan as it went against the traditional rights and conditions of the lordship. It also didn't take into account the unique character of Simon Fraser, son of Lord Lovat's grand uncle Thomas Beaufort, who would stop at nothing to get the title he came to believe was his.

In hindsight it would seem that a simple and straightforward solution would have been to marry Lord Lovat's daughter, also called Amelia, to Simon Fraser, but by that time Lord Murray, who was Amelia's guardian and had been given the gift of the ward for her, detested Fraser and the feeling was mutual. In the opinion of W.C. Mackenzie F.S.A., author of the *Life and Times of Simon Fraser* (1908), opposition to this match affected the whole course of British history in the first half of the eighteenth century.

According to Fraser, whose own memoirs are obviously written with a distinct bias, his conflict with Murray began in 1695 when Lord Murray requested Simon come to a meeting at his home at Huntingtower. In the previous year Murray had been appointed colonel of a regiment of foot soldiers which was to be raised in Scotland, consisting of thirteen companies, and as such he had significant influence in making appointments to this regiment. Fraser claimed he was in Perth at this time, at the invitation of Lord Murray's father, the marquis, and had been asked to pass the winter there with another of the marquis' sons, Mungo, to study maths. According to Fraser the marquis was at this point estranged from his eldest son, Lord Murray, as he considered him a traitor to his sovereign for having accepted the appointment as colonel of a regiment of King William. In contrast, Fraser claimed the marquis very much respected the loyalty shown by him to King James II.

Fraser then detailed how, as part of a plot to deceive him during the meeting at Huntingtower, Lord Murray claimed to be a supporter of King James, and forced Simon to commit to raising a regiment of Frasers who would be loyal supporters of James and could be used by Murray the following summer. However, when Murray was then appointed Secretary of State for Scotland in King William's government, he went back on his word and in a sudden desire to show his support for the king, he not only didn't give Fraser the charge of a company as promised, he also forced the regiment Fraser had raised to make the oath of abjuration, which demanded officials swear an oath of loyalty to the Protestant succession and deny the Catholic James II and his son their claim to the throne.

Describing a heated meeting which took place later with Lord Murray, Fraser wrote:

The Colonel [Murray] upon this acknowledged, that he had been at that time very much inclined to King James's party: but since he had been much enlightened upon the subject and that it was his regard to the welfare of the Protestant religion that induced him to be faithful to King William. Simon replied without any circumlocution, that what induced him to be faithful to King William was the appointment of Secretary of State: adding that if he pressed him a moment longer upon this subject he would declare to all the world that Lord Murray had engaged him in his regiment for the service of James. Thus, it was that this nobleman now lord Atholl and who is at this hour the favourite hero and the grand pillar of the court of St Germain was the first and the only man who obliged the officers of the Scottish army to take the oath of abjuration against King James.[1]

It was the combination of a refusal by Murray to grant Fraser a captaincy in one of the companies of his regiment, and his family being treated as poor relations in the marriage contract of their clan chief which seems to have affronted Fraser beyond endurance. His memoirs are colourful, impassioned and highly entertaining, but embittered and utterly prejudiced. His loathing of Murray is apparent on every page where he is mentioned, and on this occasion his narrative of events was clearly written to tarnish Murray's reputation, portraying him as someone who couldn't be trusted and who would switch sides at any offer of advancement. Written with the benefit of hindsight, he implicates Murray in every Jacobite plot going, but the picture he paints doesn't ring true with what was going on in Murray's life at the time. For example, later in 1696 there was a rumoured plot to assassinate the king, but far from being suspected as one of the the ringleaders, Murray was sent by the king to Edinburgh to examine the people concerned. Meanwhile, of course, Fraser portrays his own actions as reasonable, justified and loyal, even heroic on occasion!

At the start of 1696, Hugh, Lord Lovat, was invited to London to be presented to King William by Lord Murray, who was now Earl of Tullibardine and clearly in favour with the king. Simon offered to accompany his chief and kept company with him for the visit. However, despite later being ordered back to Scotland by Tullibardine, who had been sent north to investigate the rumoured plot, Lovat wrote he intended to resign his commission in favour of his cousin, Simon Fraser, and instead both stayed in London (Simon was Hugh's first cousin once removed). Most officer posts in the army and cavalry were obtained by paying for a commission instead of promotion by merit or seniority. The colonel of the regiment had to approve the purchase and therefore held a significant amount of influence in the process.

It was during this stay in London that Lovat then revoked his marriage contract and signed a disposition in favour of his grand-uncle, should he die without a male heir. His grand uncle was Thomas Fraser of Beaufort, head of a cadet branch of the Fraser clan and Simon's father. Sadly, Lovat's baby son John had recently died, as had a previous son, and so the likelihood of there being a direct male heir was gone. This, as far as Simon and his father were concerned, had hastened the need of a change of heart from the chief. According to Simon, however, the reason for the change of heart was because Lord Lovat had been shown plainly that Lord Murray had 'made a jest of him', bringing him down to London at Lovat's own vast expense only to be denied what had been promised. Fraser alleged that Murray had promised he would resign the command of his regiment in Lovat's favour as, having been made Secretary of State, there was no example of anyone retaining a position as colonel while holding that office; Murray had then claimed he couldn't fulfil this promise because the king wanted him to retain command till the threat of invasion had passed:

> Lord Lovat was so deeply impressed with the treachery of the family of Atholl, as well respecting him, as respecting the Kings William and James that, intreating his cousin Simon to return with him to his own seat of Lovat he swore that he would never see the Marquis of Athol nor any of the young lords, his children who he had hitherto supported from year to year they not having so much as a maintenance in their own family. Impressed at the same time with the tender affection of the laird of Beaufort [Simon] and the resolution he manifested never to abandon him, Lord Lovat declared that he regarded him as his own son.[2]

This all seems very poignant and heart-warming, but also highly convenient. Fraser's memoirs make very entertaining reading, but can hardly be relied on as an impartial account.

The change in title deeds was of immediate importance to both families when, after returning to Scotland in September 1696, Lord Lovat died in Perth. He had been ill for some time, including during his stay in London. Lady Katherine was in London during this time and commented to her husband:

> Oh he is a sad creature and keeps the worst of company, he has nothing to do now he has dimeted, so he'll stay here and spend of his own and take his pleasures a while. If there could be any way falen upon to get him to Scotland it would be happy for him for I am afraid he fall into some inconveniency.[3]

Fraser blamed the fact his Lord was visiting too many taverns in the city 'where he contracted his distemper',[4] on the disappointments he had suffered at the hands of the Atholl family, who were therefore the cause of his illness and who also failed to look after him at his death.

As the new male heir, Thomas Beaufort immediately claimed the title Lord Lovat and possession of the estate, while Simon Fraser styled himself Master of Lovat and therefore next in line. In Fraser's opinion the rights of the house of Lovat for time immemorial had always been in favour of the male heirs in exclusion of the female, this was incontestable and no man in the north of Scotland would think the marquis of Atholl could challenge it. Obviously the Murray family thought differently; as far as they were concerned the eldest daughter assumed the title while the widow Amelia, now dowager Lovat, held the estates.

Initially, Lord Tullibardine made an attempt to win Fraser round, by inviting him to join him for a drink with some companions in Edinburgh and persuade him to sign away his rights to the property and honours of Lovat, in return for a regiment and an income. Of course Fraser refused and, given their recent history, it seems naive of Tullibardine to think he would go for this, even with the weight of lawyers (the companions) as back-up to his argument.

This firmness and spirit threw the Lord commissioner into a violent passion. He exclaimed with a furious tone; I have always known you for an obstinate insolent rascal. I do not know what should hinder me from cutting off your ears or from throwing you into a dungeon, and bringing you to the gallows as your treason against the government so richly deserves.[5]

Fraser left the meeting, but not without being tempted first to run Tullibardine through with his sword, the only thing that stopped him, apparently, being the fact Tullibardine had no weapon. Fraser declared:

I do not know what hinders me knave and coward as you are, from running my sword through your body, You are well known for a poltroon and if you had one grain of courage you would never have chosen your ground in the midst of your guards to insult a gentleman of a better house and of a more honourable birth than your own.[6]

This language became fairly commonplace between the two over the next years and explains why the simple solution to the issue, i.e. to marry Simon to the heiress Amelia, was never considered an option.

Inevitably the division over who had the right claim to the title and property quickly caused problems and disorder in the area. In September 1697 Amelia the dowager Lovat wrote to her brother from Beaufort, to explain that an order for arresting 'old Beaufort' (Thomas Fraser) would be difficult to enforce as they couldn't trust the officers or the people around them. She also explained that in addition to this they were having difficulty getting rents collected, as tenants were refusing to pay anything till they had decided who had the best right to it.[7] At the same time the Marquis had arranged for the heir (also called Amelia) to marry – in accordance with the original agreement – a Fraser (Alexander Master of Saltoun) and in order to pursue this Lord Saltoun, his father, accompanied by Mungo Murray, visited the dowager Lovat at Castle Dounie, near Beauly in Inverness-shire. Returning to Inverness on 6 October 1697, however, they were attacked by Simon Fraser and a group of loyal Stratherrick men in the woods of Bunchrew.

Fraser later claimed that Lord Saltoun had been warned by letter not to meddle in the affair but had chosen to ignore this advice, and consequently Fraser had been forced to act in order to up hold his own honour and that of the house of Fraser. The Lords Saltoun and Murray, were taken to Finellan House and held prisoner for six or seven days, during which time Fraser erected gallows near the window of the room they were confined in, and on which he threatened to hang them unless the marriage arrangement was called off. At the same time, he sent a number of his followers to Beaufort to prevent the dowager Lovat from sending for help from her father and brothers, effectively holding her prisoner in her own home. The two lords were later removed from their original prison and kept on an island called Eilan Aigas in the river Beauly; shortly after this, however, Lord Saltoun became ill, and fearing he may actually die – which was a step too far – Fraser set him free.

Law and order in the area at this time was in the hands of Colonel John Hill, the governor at Fort William. This was the same Colonel Hill who MacIan of Glencoe had first attempted to make his submission to on 30 December 1691 before what became the tragic massacre in 1692. Hill was considered a more tolerant officer than most; his method of governance was more for negotiation than use of force. In 1691, to assist MacIan, Hill had given him a letter explaining the confusion over his making his submission on time, but it had had no effect. Hill had also delayed giving the order to carry out the massacre hoping it would be countermanded, but eventually did tell his second-in-command, Lieutenant Colonel James Hamilton, to act on the orders he had received from his commander-in-chief. Hill was cleared of being an accessory by the Royal Commission in 1695, but perhaps this incident and his involvement in it influenced the way he handled the Beaufort affair because he seems to have been easily duped by Fraser into believing the dowager Lovat didn't need help. Hill's inaction infuriated Lord Tullibardine, but more significantly, allowed Fraser the opportunity to take his next step to ensure for certain that the title would ultimately be his. But this was a step further than anyone imagined he would take, as he decided he himself would marry the dowager Lovat and consummate the act, whether she agreed or not.

On the morning of either the 19 or 20 October 1697, accompanied by two Frasers, the Rev. Robert Munro and a piper, Simon entered the chambers of the dowager Lovat, forced her ladies to leave and performed a wedding ceremony, including consummation, during which the piper played outside the room to drown out the cries of the bride. Whether this is what actually happened, and whether she was a willing bride or not, is debatable. Fraser denied it, both the marriage and the incident, saying, 'he had no reason therefore to commit the smallest violence upon a widow, who was old enough to be his mother, dwarfish in her person and deformed in her shape',[8] but after the countrywide backlash, he was unlikely to admit it.

Fraser's denial was contradicted by both the local populace and his father. In November Murray of Dollery wrote: 'Other people make it their business to spread about that my Lady Lovett went willingly with him to the hills and now adheres to the marriage.'[9] While the 10th Lord Lovat, Fraser's father, wrote to the Earl of Argyll:

> ... we have gained a considerable advantage by my eldest son's being married to the dowager of Lovat; and if it please God they live some years together our circumstances will be very good. Our enemies are so galled at it, that there is nothing that malice or cruelty can invent but they design and practice against us ... Also they have my son and his complices guilty of rape, though his wife was married to him by a minister and they have lived always since as man and wife.[10]

At the trial held later in Fraser's absence, both of Lady Lovat's servants testified to the incident and stated she had been forced, that Captain Simon had 'pulled off her petticoats and sought a knife from Hugh Munro to cut her stays and because he had none the Captain ordered Fraser of Kinmonavie to cut the stays with his dirk and then they through the lady on the bed.'[11] When the servant Amelia Rioche,

… was going away, she heard my lady cry but the bagpipes did play all the time in the next room to my lady's chamber that her cries might not be heard … The next morning she went into the lady's chamber and saw her head hang over the bed and nothing upon it except a handkerchief … did see all the lady's face swollen and she spoke nothing but gave her a broad look.[12]

The second servant also reported seeing her lady's face swollen and that she had frequently fallen in a swoon during the incident. Also Robertson of Straloch testified that Lady Lovat had begged he take her 'out of this place either dead of alive',[13] also observing her face was swollen.

Lady Lovat's father, the marquis, and her elder brother Tullibardine were horrified at such an assault on their relative and their name. Tullibardine, who was in London and receiving delayed updates, reacted with fury, writing to Sir John Hill in November 1697:

… it appears you have been grossly mistaken in your intelligence, but it seems you have relied on young Beaufort's answer to your letter, with whom it had been fitter you had treated by the sword than by your pen, after your owning that you had account of his convocating such a number of armed men without the King's authority, and had committed such barbarous actions with them. As for what my sister did write considering she was a prisoner you had no reason to delay sending a partie … I will deal so plainly with you as to tell you I will inform the King of this matter so soon as it pleases God to return him to this kingdom.[14]

Orders from the privy council in Edinburgh were issued for troops from Lords Carmichael and Forbes' regiments to march into Fraser country, and Lord James Murray (another son of the Marquis) raised an army of Atholl men to support the sheriff in the area. From Edinburgh, Patrick, Earl of Marchmont, King's Commissioner to the Scottish Parliament, wrote to Tullibardine:

Now I only tell your lordship that if a daughter of mine was in your sister's room, I am sure I could not be more heartily concerned to prosecute those who have done this injury than I am. I am hopeful the course the council has taken shall answer our expectations and we shall quickly have a good account of it. If we do not in this case show a notable example of the justice and diligence of the government we should be very much to blame.[15]

It appears on the arrival of such a force, including by this point the best of Colonel Hill's men, the Frasers had initially fled and allowed the dowager Lovat to leave Inverness-shire for her family home in Dunkeld. According to Fraser before the arrival of regiments, 'with tears in his eyes' he had persuaded his father the Lord Lovat to retire to Skye, to his brotherinlaw, the head of the clan Macleod. While the members of the Fraser clan professed their undying loyalty to the Master of Lovat he then claimed all damage inflicted on the area was done only by forces led by the Murrays and had any other of the forces attacked he could, if he had wanted, defeated them without any problems.

For some time the Murrays doggedly pursued the Frasers, sending out word they were to be captured dead or alive, but every attempt was limited by both the weather and Clan Fraser loyalty to their chief and the Master of Lovat. The Murrays' severe actions certainly didn't win them any favours in the area and probably went a long way to securing support for Fraser. However, the brothers James Murray, Lord Nairne and Mungo Murray were carrying out the orders of their father the marquis and elder brother Lord Tullibardine, who were determined to capture the 'villain of villaines' for the sake of family honour. At one stage the marquis headed the search himself and was very disheartened by what he came up against, as he felt no one in the area could be trusted.

Eventually, having evaded capture on several occasions and getting the better of the Murray brothers on another, Fraser made the decision that because Atholl had paid for villains to assassinate him, it would be safer for both him and the whole clan if he also retreated to Skye.

In 1698 Lord Lovat and his son Simon were cited for trial for treason and other crimes. They were tried in absentia, which was unique, as previously the law had stated trials for treason could not be held in the absence of the accused. This law had even gone as far as holding trials of the recently deceased accused with their corpses present, as in the case of the Ruthven brothers after the Gowrie Conspiracy in 1600. (The Ruthvens were the previous owners of the home of Lord Tullibardine, the now renamed, Huntingtower).

The Frasers were found guilty,

> ... to be execute to death, demeaned as traitors, and to undergo the pains of treason, and utter punishment, appointed by the laws of the realm, at such times and places and in such manner as the said lords should appoint: and ordain their name, fame, memory and honours to be extinct and their arms to be riven forth, and delete out of the books of arms so that their prosperity may never have place for be able hereafter to bruik or joice any honours offices titles or dignities within the realm in time coming.[16]

However, not everyone was comfortable with this verdict. The Earl of Seafield, who had been made Secretary of State at the same time as Tullibardine, wrote to William Carstares (Scottish chaplain and adviser to King William and who had considerable influence with him), 'I cannot indeed justify Fraser in his proceedings; but yet the rendering of so many men desperate is not at all in the interest of the government.'[17] Lord Lovat had also written for help to the Earl of Argyll, claiming Tullibardine had planned to marry his eldest son, Johny, to the young heiress Amelia which, if it came to pass, would cause much disturbance and bloodshed in that part of the country. Argyll could do nothing to help the Frasers at the trial, but did invite Simon to London to plead for a pardon and, in time, the 2nd Duke of Argyll would play a significant role in getting the sentence remitted. At this time, however, Simon, who was now 11th Lord Lovat after the death of his father in 1699, fled from London to France and the court in exile of King James, where he would continue his efforts to both blacken the Atholl name and find a way to claim his inheritance.

Throughout the whole episode Tullibardine had been increasingly frustrated due to the delay in receiving news while he was in London and having to rely on others to carry out his instructions. This had changed dramatically however when, after returning to Scotland, he was arrested in Edinburgh in August 1698 for allegedly attempting to strike Lord Ross of Balnagoun, a friend of Simon Fraser's.

The order for arrest had come from Patrick, Earl of Marchmont, the King's Commissioner to the Scottish Parliament, who wrote to the king from Edinburgh that,

> ... it is like, your majesty may have heard a complaint against me, that I commanded the Earl of Tullibardine to be under arrest in his chamber, which I did, upon a heavy complain of abuse committed by him and his brother on the Laird of Balnagoun, a gentleman of the best quality in the kingdom ...I know your Majesty will reserve an ear for me and I doubt not to satisfy you with my reason besides that of preserving the peace and preventing bloodshed, while the parliament was sitting, there being in town an abundance of Highlanders of the Earl of Tullibardine's men and the Laird of Balnagoun's carrying swords, daggers and side pistols upon them as their manner is.[18]

Indignation was expressed by the Murray family and followers at Marchmont's lack of loyalty, considering it had been Tullibardine who had recommended him to his post and that Balnagoun was being helped by the old Murray family's rival the Duke of Argyll, who was also advising the Master of Lovat. As ever, rivalries continued to bubble below the surface.

Tullibardine's account of the incident was very different. During the Fraser trial when tempers were riding high, Tullibardine claimed a heated discussion had taken place during which he had interrogated Balnagoun as to why he hadn't acted to try and save both his sister and Lord Saltoun during the recent episodes. In reply Balnagoun had stated that he had the greatest respect for the lord's sister and had visited her when she was married to her first husband. But the words 'first husband' had enraged Tullibardine as, in his opinion, it implied she had had a second husband, i.e Simon Fraser, and if that was the implication, Tullibardine thought, 'you deserve to be beat for such an expression to her own brother.'[19] However, he then claimed that Balnagoun had apologised immediately so he said he would think no more of it.

Naturally, Lord Tullibardine received the full support of both his own family and that of his wife following his arrest. Katherine was appalled that her husband could have been accused of such an act, in her opinion the accuser was a known liar and to her, 'one might have expected the commissioner wold have belived my lord as well as such a person but times are changed.'[20] She immediately wrote to her brother James, the 4th Duke of Hamilton declaring that Tullibardine had been confined to his chamber 'for a crime he is abslutly inosent of',[21] and urging Hamilton to, 'be not slow in showing yourself very active in this affair I know you can doe if you wish I do not doubt but you will doe all in your power.'[22] In a second letter she wrote, 'let great cair be taken that it be not falsly in the prints, there is nothing that has inclined anybody here to give the least credit to those storys of his beating the man.'[23] To Charles, Lord Selkirk, who was a gentlemen of the bedchamber to the king so with direct access, she wrote: 'I expect dear brother you will not at this time be idle but lay yourself to vindicate my Lord.'[24] She also persuaded a third brother, Basil, to go to Edinburgh to help Lord Tullibardine and his brothers, who were also accused and it is from his letters, corresponding with the Duke of Hamilton to keep him up to date that we hear how the trial progressed.

According to Basil it was clear that the witnesses had agreed some sort of made-up story which, when questioned on, 'they were confounded and contradicted themselves.'[25] He relates one particular instance of the trial: a witness was asked if he knew who Lord Tullibardine's brothers James and Edward Murray were, and the witness agreed that he did. This witness was then asked to look about him and point to them. There were a lot of people around Basil including Lord James who was standing right in front of him but, Basil wrote, the witness, 'after much consideration he pointed to me and called me Lord Edward and then seeing all laughing at him, to mend it he said I was Lord James though he was standing just beside me', when everyone laughed again.'[26] Also to the Duke of Hamilton, Tullibardine wrote: 'the very witnesses that ware chosen to prove against me are the persons that have vindicated me more then anything.'[27]

Lord Tullibardine was acquitted, which he was relieved to report to his parents in November 1698:

> Before the Earl of Argyll came to town I was very anxious to have this affair ended, and indeed I had then the majority of the Council for me, but the chancelor delayed it, but nothing to their advantage, but very far to the conterar, for the dispositions of the witnesses are so gross, that all our enemies are ashamed, and I am come off with honour.[28]

The truth of what had happened to Lady Lovat is difficult to resolve, and a letter from the marquis to his son in December 1697 does raise another possibility. In it he says:

> I wish you wou'd writt a kind letter to your poor sister, who is in a very melancholy condition. Your dear mother within these 4 or 5 days has been in such a condition, that I never was so frightened in my life for her, upon discovery concerning your sister, which I will not trouble you with now.[29]

There is a possibility Lady Lovat could have been pregnant, or at least thought she was, and this would account for some of her actions as she is reported at one stage to have wanted to stay with Fraser.[30] However the marquis also wrote how Lady Lovat was persuaded by Straloch, a captain in one of Murray's companies,

> … to yeild to all that base man's proposals & even to swear to it, which made her despair because she thought he wou'd not said so if it had not been the sentiements of all her relations, whom she knew intirly trusted him and this he did no only publickly, but even in private to her, when she called him to that purpose. This was most surprising to us all of anything we heard yet.[31]

Straloch's out of character comments may account for her thinking she had to stay with Fraser, but this doesn't explain the discovery which upset her mother so much.

Ultimately however, it was Tullibardine who took care of his sister and her children. Initially the dowager Lovat stayed at Dunkeld with her parents, but then lived in the Murray property in the centre of Perth. For this she was clearly grateful, and it demonstrated the sense of duty and responsibility John Murray always felt to all of his family. To her sister-in-law, Katherine, Lady Lovat wrote: 'Tho I bee the most unfortunate creature ever was, yett I have the comfort in my extrem misere to be ownd by such kind relations as my dearest sister and brother, which is God's goodness to me and not any disart of my own.'[32]

Despite Tullibardine's acquittal and the verdict against Fraser ensuring he was now an outlaw and had to flee the country, the feud between them was far from over and it wasn't long before it would raise its head again.

Chapter 4

The Duke of Atholl

T he start of the eighteenth century saw a series of high profile deaths which radically altered the state of play in the country and for the Murray family. It began in 1700 when the Duke of Gloucester, Princess Anne's only son to survive infancy, died aged 11. As William and Mary had had no children, Gloucester had been second in line to the throne after his mother and had, while he lived, secured the Protestant succession. His death meant measures needed to be put in place to ensure the throne went to anyone other than the Catholic Stuarts. The strongest Protestant contender was Princess Sophia, the youngest daughter of Charles I's sister and her son, the Elector George Ludwig of Hanover. In fact, there were many other more direct heirs, but all were Roman Catholic. To secure this Hanoverian succession by law, an Act of Settlement was passed by Parliament in England, which provided that the crown would pass to Princess Sophia and her Protestant descendants and ensured Roman Catholics were excluded. The Act, however, didn't receive support in Scotland where ministers were unimpressed at not being consulted and at the exclusion of the Scottish Stuart line.

On 6 September the following year James VII died in St Germain. His son, the 13-yearold Prince of Wales, was proclaimed King James III and VIII of England, Scotland and Ireland and against the advice of some of his ministers, his accession was recognised by Louis XIV of France. Then in 1702 King William, who had fallen from his horse which tripped on a mole hill, also died. Jacobites later would raise a toast to 'the wee gentleman in the black velvet waistcoat', in recognition of the role played in the succession by this mole. James VII's second daughter Anne, sister of William's wife Mary, succeeded to the throne and in a round of new appointments made Lord Tullibardine a privy counsellor and Lord Privy Seal for Scotland.

In February 1703 Tullibardine's mother, the marchioness, died at Dunkeld, followed only three months later by the death of her husband, the marquis. Ever the dutiful son, Tullibardine left his parliamentary affairs in order to attend the funeral, writing to his wife from Edinburgh, 'you cannot imagine what difficulties I have had to leave this place to doe the last duty to my father, which, conterar to the advice of all my friends here, I am resolved, God willing to perform to him.'[1]

Due to the death of his father, in quick succession Tullibardine became Marquis of Atholl and then on 30 June 1703 was elevated to the higher status of Duke of Atholl, Marquis of Tullibardine, Earl of Strathtay and Strathardle, Viscount of Balquidder Glenalmond and Glenlyon and Lord Murray Balvaird and Gask. The royal charter read:

> ... in as much as we are royally aware of the good faith, zeal and affection of our well beloved kinsman and councillor of our ancient kingdom of Scotland, for us and our authority and that he comes from the royal line of Stewarts, and that the family of Atholl is in one of the most noble and ancient of the said kingdom of Scotland and that because of its most famous actions for us and our predecessors throughout many centuries it has been adorned not only the highest titles of honour and dignity but also with office and appointments of the highest trust which they have always fulfilled with notable honour and unblemished good faith and that the said marquis has preserved and increased the honour and dignity of his said family by his most noble, virtuous and superior conduct.[2]

On 5 February 1704 he was made a Knight of the Thistle.

Now one of the most prominent figures in Scottish politics and society, it was significant that in response to the Act of Settlement, Atholl gave his support to the Act of Security. In his opinion any diminution of the role of a Scottish peer was not to be tolerated, a view he was to re-enforce during negotiations for the Union. The Act of Security stated that unless Scotland was granted freedom of trade,

Parliament would settle the succession on a different monarch from England. It read:

> ... the successor to the imperial crown of this realm and to settle the succession thereof upon the heirs of the said successor's body, the said successor and the heirs of the successor's body being always of the royal line of Scotland and of the true Protestant religion, providing always that the same be not successor to the crown of England, unless that, in this present session of parliament or any other session of this or any ensuing parliament during her majesty's reign, there be such conditions of government settled and enacted as may secure the honour and sovereignty of this crown and kingdom, the freedom, frequency and power of parliaments, the religion, liberty and trade of the nation from English or any foreign influence, with power to the said meeting of estates to add such further conditions of government as they shall think necessary.[3]

From the English Parliament's point of view, this Act opened up the possible return of a Stuart king to the throne, which couldn't be allowed to happen. It also infuriated the Duke of Queensberry, the Secretary of State for Scotland and the English ministers because in addition, the Scottish Parliament threatened to withdraw support (which meant soldiers) for the Wars of the Spanish Succession. It was perhaps Atholl's support for the Act which allowed Queensberry to be so easily duped by Simon Fraser, now Lord Lovat, into believing Atholl was corresponding with Jacobites in France and to use this evidence to bring him down.

Lord Lovat was at this time heading to Scotland from France, to lay the groundwork and gather evidence of there being enough support for a Jacobite rising. He also had his own agenda, however, as his modus operandi was always to do what he could to regain his title and estates. His timely intervention should have sent alarm bells ringing for Queensberry, who was well aware there was no love lost between Lovat and Atholl, but instead he chose to believe Lovat and presented evidence to the queen that Atholl was involved in a Jacobite plot. The

Queensberry or Scotch plot, as it was known, was betrayed by Robert Ferguson. He informed Atholl of what was happening which allowed the duke time to write to the queen showing that Queensberry had corresponded with someone outlawed in Scotland by giving Lovat a pass and protection to go to St Germain.

Lord Lovat claimed that the whole plan had been arranged by Queensberry, that when they met he had reminded Lovat of how Atholl and Hamilton had for a long time tried to deprive him of his estates, his reputation and his life and that all he, Queensberry, needed was for Lovat to report that Atholl and Hamilton had corresponded with the court in St Germain. 'The Duke of Queensberry at this time breathed the most inveterate enmity against Hamilton and Athol because they opposed the projects of that nobleman in his parliament.'[4] Lovat claimed Queensberry would have done anything to deprive these two of their power and he, Lovat, was of course delighted to help. 'With respect to Lord Athol, he was notoriously the incorrigible enemy of King James, his accumulated treasons rendered his person odious to all his majesty's faithful servants. Much less therefore was Lord Lovat bound to spare this incomparable villain, and the Duke his brother-in-law.'[5]

Queensberry was deprived of his office but in 1704, unable to escape the taint of suspicion, Atholl either resigned the post of Lord Privy Seal or had it taken from him.

My Lord – I received your Lordship's som time agoe with the accompt that her Majesty had thought fitt to dispose of the Privy Seale's place which I received with all the submission that was proper and also with much contentment being satisfied that I am guilty of nothing but preferring the Queen to her successor & my native country of Scott: to England.[6]

According to George Lockhart the episode did,

... so exasperate him against the court, that he joyn'd entirely with the Cavaliers: and from being a friend to the revolution and an admirer of King William, he became all of a sudden a violent

Jacobite, and took all methods to gain the favour and confidence of the Cavaliers ... and thereupon affected extremely to be the head of that party and outrival the Duke of Hamilton.[7]

Clearly resentful of the way he had been treated and short of money (he was owed salaries consisting of three terms, expenses for his travel and arrears due to him as Colonel) Atholl was also increasingly anti-union, but that didn't necessarily mean he was Jacobite, in fact it is difficult to know precisely what he thought. That he was anti-Union and anti-English in politics can't be disputed, but that didn't mean he was also against the crown or that he would ally himself with James III.

In 1705 the English Parliament passed the Alien Act in retaliation to the Act of Security. This meant Scottish nationals owning estates in England would be treated as foreigners, which endangered their legal rights and perhaps more significantly, put an embargo on Scottish exports including linen, cattle and coal to England and the English colonies. There was a provision, however, which stated the Act would be suspended if the Scottish Parliament entered into negotiations for a union.

This, of course, did nothing to enhance Scottish opinion of the English Parliament and went some way to hardening the attitude of those opposed to union. James Murray who was looking for accommodation for Atholl in Edinburgh in September 1706 wrote, 'the general talk of the toun seems to be against the union.'[8] But the Dowager Duchess Anne Hamilton was of the opinion in the same month that 'treators' were busy 'perverting the people to ther being for this incorporating union.'[9] In October, while in Edinburgh himself to attend what was to be the last Scottish Parliament before the Union, Atholl shared his wife's misgivings about the treaty and was convinced that he had been wrong to have concerned himself over public affairs before, as they 'were trifling compared to this.'[10] The Duke of Hamilton regretted that disorder in Edinburgh had meant the presence of military guards was now deemed necessary, and suspected this was a step taken deliberately by the government to prevent free discussion of the treaty.[11]

Atholl was offered a bribe in the form of payment of arrears of his salary to absent himself from the parliamentary sessions to discuss the treaty: 'I have reason to beleeve ther is a project on foot of paying your Grace what is due by the publick on condition you stay away from parliament.'[12] This had been proposed by the duke's brother the Earl of Dunmore, who told the messenger that 'such a thing might be brought about providing they were secured of your Grace staying at home and that he thought your Grace should consider the interest of your numerous family.'[13] But Katherine, writing on her husband's instructions, rejected the proposal: 'my Lord, who says it seems they think they'll get him very cheap that would put him off with giving him his owne, which he expects to get from the justice of the parliament.'[14]

The attempts to silence him didn't dampen the duke's ardour; while discussions went ahead in the parliament for the selection of commissioners to treat for union, Atholl entered a protestation, in response to the Alien Act, which was defeated. Throughout the debates on the articles of the Union he was a leading opponent. Before the vote on article 1 of the treaty, he handed in a protestation against an incorporating union, voted against this article and then consistently against the majority of the treaty provisions. He also supported others' protestations, including that from Lord Belhaven on the Church of Scotland, one by the Earl Marischal and another by Lord Annandale.[15] On 7 January 1707 Atholl handed in a protestation against article 22 on the future Scottish representation of forty-five members in the House of Commons and sixteen peers in the House of Lords. In it he stated:

> ... and so her majestie deprived of her born councellors and the peers of their birthright, and wheras they are at present a hundred and sixty in number, they are, by this article, reduced to sixteen, which sixteen are to be joined with the house of lords in England, whose number at present consists of above an hundred and eighty, wherby it is plain that the Scots peers share in the legislative and judicative powers in the Brittish parliament is very unequall with that of the English, tho' the one be representatives

of as independent and free a nation as the other, and is therfore a plain forfeiture of the peerage of this kingdome.[16]

In keeping with his character and status, Atholl was anxious to uphold the status of the Scottish elite and prevent any lessening of the prestige associated with being part of the Scottish aristocracy. His opponents accused him of feeling insecure due to the competition he would face from the English lords and he was clearly affronted by the idea that a peer of Scotland would be seen as having less worth than that of England.

It is likewise contrair to the honor and true interest of her majesty and the monarchie to suppress the estate of peers who have formerly been the great supporters of the monarchie. And, it is dishonorable and disgracefull for this kingdome that the peers therof shall only have rank and precedencie next after the peers of the like order and degree in England, without regaird to their antiquity or the dates of their patents.[17]

But at the final vote on 16 January 1707, when the complete treaty was ratified, Atholl was not present; his absence explained by the sudden death of his wife and 'retirement to his own estates'.[18] Although some see this as an excuse and as an example of his sitting on the fence, it is impossible to believe her sudden death didn't genuinely have a devastating effect on him.

Atholl's outspoken opinions, and his being a leading opponent of the treaty, had made him a prime candidate for Jacobite interest, however, and it wasn't long before he became embroiled in the next plot. Unfortunately, crucial evidence on this is missing; there is a distinct lack of correspondence in the Blair Archives, so it can be safe to assume it was intentionally destroyed at the time to avoid any incrimination. Many references are made to Atholl being a suspect Jacobite, but noble families had to be pragmatic at this time. It was a period of political and economic turmoil and it was difficult to predict which way the wind would blow; after all, in the last twenty years there had been four different monarchies and the succession was not a certainty, although it's easy now to look back and think it was.

That there was a plot is without doubt, but what part, if any, Atholl played in it is more difficult to pin down. Louis XIV viewed the unrest and bad feeling over the union as an ideal opportunity to make a move and sent the agent Colonel Nathaniel Hooke to Scotland to gauge opinion. Hooke landed in the Northern part of Scotland in March 1707 and quickly came to the conclusion that Atholl's support would be very important to the success of any plan. He was told by the Constable of Scotland, the Earl of Errol, that,

> ... the Duke was very opinionated, but a man of great probity, and that his word is invoilable, and may be depended upon; that he is haughty and passionate; that he is very powerful in several counties, and can raise 9 battalions among among his vassals, of 600 men each, armed, regimented, and disciplined ... that the Duke could arm a great number, and that by the interest of his friends he is absolutely the most powerful Lord in Scotland.[19]

Hooke made several attempts to meet Atholl but it appears he never actually did, the closest time being prevented by both becoming ill. Even Lockhart wrote: 'I cannot indeed say that he had a personal interview with the Duke of Athol.'[20] However, the main message Hooke got from Atholl was that, despite what he had heard (that they were in opposition with each other), Hooke should not neglect the Duke of Hamilton as 'he would willingly forget what had passed and join with him [the Duke of Hamilton] in the common cause, the moment he should see him fairly embarked in it; but not before.'[21]

Hooke retuned to France convinced there was sufficient support for James. The Memorial of the Scottish Lords to the French King, which he took with him said: 'The whole nation will rise upon the arrival of it's King; he will become master of Scotland without any opposition and the present government will be entirely abolished.'

In the spring of 1708 James VIII left Dunkirk with the support of his French allies, but as was always the way with Jacobite rebellions, the weather deteriorated and James became ill with measles. The Jacobite ships were out-manoeuvred by the Royal Navy who, led by Sir George Byng, forced the French to retreat, without James setting foot on Scottish soil.

The government's reaction was to order the arrest of several leading Scottish nobles suspected of being involved. This included Lord Nairne and the Duke of Gordon being sent to London; deposit bonds for surety of good behaviour had to be paid by Breadalbane, Errol, Nithsdale, Strathmore and Marishal. On 19 March, Lieutenant Campbell of the Lord Carmichael's Dragoons was sent to Blair with orders from General Leven to take the Duke of Atholl to Edinburgh. His was to seize the duke on suspicion of high treason and treasonable practices.[22] The duke refused to go but Lieutenant Campbell returned on 10 April with a detachment of dragoons and, claiming he was too ill to travel, Atholl was held under house arrest.

There is a lot written about whether this illness was genuine or feigned, most assuming it was very convenient that Atholl's varying health coincided with political events. But throughout his life the duke suffered often, with a variety of illnesses which were genuine and severe and were commented on by his concerned wives and relations. These included frequent bouts of violent headaches, fevers and vomiting. His mother, the marchioness, had written to him in 1690 about his 'jaundice and vapours', recommending a cure which included fifteen or seventeen slaters (woodlice),

> ... put in a thin linen cloute & then steeped in 3 spoon-fulls of brandie or aqua vita all night and next morning bruise the cloute they are in and take a spoonfull or 2 fasting in a morning and as much at 4 o'clock and this for 3 daeis.[23]

Katherine frequently expressed her concern about his health both in her letters and by praying to God to help him through his illnesses. In 1716 his second wife Mary Ross described one of the episodes of his 'indisposition' in detail to his son James, asking him to consult physicians in London about what course of action should be taken. In her opinion, his trouble arises from his weakness and indigestion of his stomach which rasis violent pains in his head which begins with excessive heat all over his head and then later above his right eye which seldom leaves him without vomittings … he's also frequently very hott his whole body but especially his hands as if he were in a fever … the pain always makes him drousie tho sleep does not allway cure the pain but the excesive heat is what I fear most and I must tell your lordship that I fear itt may be the forerunner of apoplexies which … dangerous fitts.[24]

Obviously, it would be difficult to confirm whether this was definitely the case in 1708. However, in January that year Dr John Murray from Perth had prescribed a variety of medicines for the duke including 'the bitter drink', and the 'Jesuit's powder'.[25] The doctor gave lengthy instructions of the best way to administer these medicines and mentioned he had had to visit the duke's children in Perth, presumably at Huntingtower, who had also been ill. He was pleased to report that George was then fine and Charles improving too. In correspondence from 1709 Margaret Nairne also referred to the duke's illness during this period, but she would be unlikely to hint his illness was fake. In late October 1707 Breadalbane had also referred to the duke being ill, as had Nathanial Hooke: 'the Duke of Athol, who is also of a very tender condition.'[26]

Before the end of April 1708 Captain Charles Stewart arrived with a company from the Laird of Grant's regiment and took possession of the castle. He verified that the duke was ill, or at least for the most part kept to his bed: 'he looks very thin of his body and all the people about him belives him to be very ill.'[27] Doctors letters attested to the duke's health not being good for the previous twelve months, and continued for the next few weeks to confirm he was not improving. By June, however, the strictures of his confinement were relaxed as his children, physicians, and servants were allowed free access without the presence of an officer, and in July he received notice that on the payment of bail he was to be set at liberty and the guard of soldiers to march to Stirling.

Aged between 13 and 23, it is inevitable these events would have had a huge effect on the Murray brothers, especially the younger two who were still at school in Perth. They couldn't have failed to have heard and taken notice of the resentful feeling in the country towards the union, and there is no doubt the children would have been well aware of their father's views. To then have had the fear of his arrest, their family home being occupied by soldiers and an uncle arrested and taken to London must inevitably have impacted on their developing opinions of government and law. This was all drama enough for any teenager to handle, but was exacerbated by the fact their home life had only recently been irrevocably changed by the death of their beloved mother and the following year was to be upset again by another tragic death in the family.

Chapter 5

Katherine – Wife, Sister, Mother

Katherine Hamilton was the second daughter of Duke William and Duchess Anne Hamilton and the Duke of Atholl's first wife. The dukedom of Hamilton was, and still is, the premier peerage in Scotland and, along with the status associated with being the eldest daughter of this family, Katherine had a number of high profile siblings. Among these were her eldest brother James, Earl of Arran (later the 4th Duke), John the Earl of Ruglen, George, the Earl of Orkney (who married Elizabeth Villiers, King William's ex-mistress), and Charles the Earl of Selkirk. Their influence extended over both the Scottish and English elite and, during negotiations for the Union, was particularly important.

When she married, Katherine was 'a tall, black haired young woman with a serious disposition.'[1] Highly respectful of her mother she aimed to emulate her in her own role as wife of a powerful Lord. Loyal, devout and conscientious, she was also at times passionate and opinionated. She stuck firmly by her principles and sought to instil the same strength of conviction and sense of duty in her children as her mother had with her.

Katherine's letters are an excellent source of material as she is honest and direct, showing her passion and strength of character whether it was in religion, family matters or politics. She was resolute in her opinions and rarely held back from telling her peers what she thought. The letters are often filled with religious references to her faith, to which she was genuinely committed, but they also show a sense of humour and interest in her world, both social and political. She wrote frequently and in return was constantly kept up to date by her family and friends. After her death there is a notable change in both the content and quantity of letters, and as a result the depth of detail as well as the sentiment is missing from the family archives; when it does then appear, however, it is perhaps more striking.

Given Katherine's high social status she was obviously much sought after in the matrimonial stakes, but wasn't forced into a union by her parents. When the Marquis of Atholl proposed his son, Lord John Murray, to her parents, it was left up to Lord Murray to impress her and he must have succeeded because the following year, 1683, they were married. From their letters to each other it is apparent that throughout their life they had a genuine love and affection for each other. They disliked being apart and were clearly happiest in each other's company in their homes in Scotland, neither particularly enjoying London. On several occasions they wrote joint letters and from their correspondence when they were apart, it is clear they communicated well on many aspects of life, agreeing in most areas, but also respecting each other's opinions if they differed, as well as providing support and understanding.

Throughout her life, Katherine's letters to her husband were very much dominated by wifely solicitude, care for his health, comfort, diet, advising on the right vehicle to use, people to accompany him, where he should stay and updating him on their children. A typical example of their relationship can be seen in a letter written by Katherine at Huntingtower on 9 November 1702:

> I have a little pain in my back with whipping Susan [their daughter] today, who struggled so that I have got a wrench. It was for throwing a great stick at her sister's head so that it was a mercy she dis not brain her; she is the likest thing to you that ever was seen which you may imagine does not make me the less fond. I think she minds me of Nanny some times. They are all very well I thank God as I am myself, but sitting in smoke from the nursery which is a great grievance, adieu dearest heart.[2]

And at times her sense of humour also comes through:

> I could not forbear laffing when your brother Will told me of Balaquen's* giving it out that he is to be Marquess of Atholl which

---

* (Patrick Stuart of Ballechin was appointed Colonel of the Atholl men by Bonnie Dundee during the first Jacobite rising in 1689.)

I assure you I feare not at all, unless popery gain the day (which I am confident it not, at least long time) and that we must resolve to part with our lives as well as fortuns, or do worst to turn papists.[3]

Similarly, John Murray's genuine concern for his wife was evident in his letters to her. In October 1700 he wrote from Edinburgh to Katherine at Huntingtower regarding the forthcoming birth of their child: 'The Duchess of Hamilton has been speaking to me of your being here when the lyes* in, which I confess I think reasonable and therefore told her I should record this desire since I am glad to have you with me on any account.'[4] Without her again in Edinburgh in 1703 he wrote: 'I am beginning already to want my dear extremely but must submit to God's ordering everything which he does in the best way and manner however it may appear a cross and contrary to our inclinations.'[5] Katherine this time had stayed at Dunkeld to look after his father who was gravely ill.

Katherine was always loyal to her husband and, as we have seen when he was arrested for supposedly striking Lord Balnagoun, it was Katherine who rallied the troops by calling on her brothers to help in his defence. In addition to the loyalty and the genuine affection Katherine clearly had for her husband, however, there is a definite strength of character in her letters which showed she had her own opinions and wasn't afraid to voice them to him. She was evidently no soft touch as can be seen in domestic matters, and was quick to point out when she thought her husband was remiss or changes needed to be made. In October 1702, for example, while Murray was in London, she wrote:

your letters come by the common packet you make them double price by putting a cover on them which I'm sure they need not for all the write that is in them and they are so ill put in the cover that its very easy to slip them out without breaking the seal and your wax as well as your ink is very bad.[6]

This is one of many instances demonstrating how involved she was in the family finances and in managing the household budgets; a skill

---

* (Due to give birth.)

she had ensured her competence in during her education at home in Hamilton. Aged 18 her father gave her £66 13s 4d and told her to keep an exact account of how she spent it, which she did – including £2 18s given to her brother's master for teaching her arithmetic.[7] When relatives shopped for her in London they were careful to have all the expenditure accounted for, as they had clearly been given instructions not to exceed the amount given, without good reason. In a description by the Countess of Dunmore of a shopping trip for a set of china, she wrote how she went to great lengths to get the type Katherine would want, but for the cheapest price to the extent that, 'if you please to call it Japan china few in Scotland will know the difference.'[8]

The family finances fluctuated during the years of their marriage and on several occasions dominated the correspondence of both John and Katherine. Investment in the Darien venture and the delayed receipt of the duke's salary as Lord Privy Seal and expenses had a direct impact on the family. During this time two of Katherine's brothers, the Earl of Selkirk and Earl of Ruglen, had loaned the duke money and by 1704 the non-payment of these debts was causing a major family rift. In June 1704 the brothers were unhappy the duke had left Edinburgh without either seeing them or even attempting to pay what was owed and hearing of this, Katherine advised her husband to resolve it quickly: 'I wish with all my heart these two debtors were pay'd for there is more clamering about whats owing them than all the debtors you owe.'[9]

However, in 1705 he still hadn't rectified this and Katherine wrote to her mother to plead her husband's case. Anne defended her sons, saying they knew it wasn't in the interest of the family to have the duke's credit broken, but implied the duke should settle the matter. Katherine had hoped her brothers would give him some relief as the Hamiltons still had the income from their Arran holdings but instead Selkirk began an action against Atholl which alarmed other creditors to act too. To limit further damage she wrote to Ruglen pleading her husband's case as she believed Ruglen was mistaken on what had been agreed over that debt. She argued that the duke had agreed to use his influence to get the debt paid by Lord Prestonhall, not to actually pay it himself. Ruglen was adamant that he had done what was expected of him in the agreement and received nothing but delays in return. However, he claimed he would, 'show you that I shall act a friendly part',[10] and take the duke's bond that it would be paid. But if Ruglen was expecting thanks from his sister for this he was very much mistaken; her reply was very critical, promising that,

> ... when at last Lord Lovat's own debts come to be transacted yours shall be the first. I assure you my Lord shall never have my advice to become debtor to any more of my brothers, he has met with so much unkind and ungentleman usage from one that I shall never desire him to trust another and since you refuse him a favour now, which I know to be in your power to doe him, I shall trouble you no more to aske it.[11]

Eventually an agreement was reached, and by the end of 1705 Selkirk had also received at least part payment of the amount due to him too. This wasn't the end of the duke's financial difficulties, however, as in 1706 he was still requesting payment of his salary, this time to the Earl of Mar, then the joint Secretary of State in London, and at the end of that year, shortly before her death, Katherine was still referring to, 'the queen's not paying you what she ows you, which has put you to so many difficulties ...'.[12]

Katherine had been essential in negotiating between the family members and without her support and perseverance it is unlikely the duke would have reached the compromise he did. Despite eventually receiving the money he was due, family finances continued to play an ever increasing role in the duke's life and that of his sons' and was to affect these relationships significantly, exacerbated, perhaps, by the fact that after 1707 Katherine was no longer there to act as negotiator.

In the same way, she was unrestrained when expressing her views to her siblings; privately, she was equally forthright when it came to commenting on her in-laws. She was clearly not impressed, for example, when her father-in-law was in Perth and didn't visit, which she considered to be a huge snub.[13] There had been a similar incident the year before, in the midst of a dispute between father and son over which should hold the office of Bailie of Regality of Atholl. While at Huntingtower in June 1699, she wrote to her husband:

> I cannot hold from telling you I take very ill your fathers going within halfe a mile of my nose and not coming in here, nor so much as sending; if you had married off the dunghill he could have used me no worse and tho I am his daughter in law his Lordship should remember there is a deaciency to be used even to her.[14]

A few months later she wrote to her mother that her parents-in-law continue to be 'the most unraisonable unjust people that I believe is on this earth.'[15] However, it was Katherine and her brother Basil who ultimately smoothed over relations between the father and son in this incident, she wrote: 'you are intyerly blamed for this and it looks very ill in a son to deal so with a father', but her support and loyalty was also touching as she added: 'dearest heart I intreat you over and over again doe not trouble your head for no body ells thinks it but him selfe and his other halfe.'[16]

Publicly, however, it was a different story. She was very respectful, and effectively fulfilled the role of a dutiful daughter-in-law, despite their obvious differences, which included her being Presbyterian while her in-laws were Episcopalian. In a letter to one of his sons in 1707 the duke wrote: 'I find I cannot but love good and religious persons of the Episcopal persuasion, since my mother was one. And cannot but love good and religious Presbyterians, since your mother was one.' He went so far as to claim the difference wasn't an issue between his wife and mother:

> These two most excellent and eminently pious persons ... tho the first was an Episcopal of the Church of England and the other a Presbyterian, yet from the time of our marriage to my mothers death, my mother and she had never the least warm debate in that account.[17]

Though they may not have actually argued about it, their difference in religion clearly was an issue for Katherine. This was expressed by her mother in 1703 when Katherine was at Dunkeld with the sick marquis, she wrote that she felt uneasy that she should be there without a minister or her husband for support. But despite this crucial difference, Katherine never used it as a pretence for disunity. In fact, as her loyalty was always with her husband first, she did her best to heal rifts between him and his family. She wrote to Margaret Nairne, for example, during the Fraser/Lovat feud to explain derogatory comments Lord Tullibardine had made of his brother's actions, i.e that they hadn't been very effective, and asked Margaret to allow her husband, Lord Tullibardine, to clear the matter up: 'I hope my Lord Nairne will ajourne his taking ill what his brother writ who will explain himself so that he'll find no reason.'[18]

Katherine's religion was very important to her and therefore had a primary role in her home life; in fact her husband wrote: 'I have sometimes thought she was rather too strict to it, for there was not one minute of the day that she did not employ either with hearing sermons, reading or writing concerning religion [referring to the Sabbath].'[19] In a diary she kept throughout most of her adult life she describes a religious experience she had at her childhood home; she wrote: 'O my soul! Remember Friday 18 November 1681 and Thursday 24th wherein the Lord thy God was pleased to give thee sweetest consolation in himself and some assurance of his reconciled countenance at Hamilton.'[20]

She read, consulted and quoted from her Bible frequently. In one instance in 1706, she tells how her husband was nearly killed when his horse was startled by the coach in which she was riding. She explained that everyone thought he would have fallen off, but he managed to get himself free only to be put in a similar situation again – from which he escaped unharmed.

Lord, let neither of forget this mercy and deliverance! That morning when I went to reed the 91ps: was the first placee fell up to me, the very first verse of it which I red over many times before I went further and the margenal note (It being a great house bible) which gave me great confidence and hope that God would be present that day.[21]

She also consulted other texts and asked Murray, while he was in London, to get her a book on John Calvin about the reformation and his life etc., as she thought it would 'be well worth the having'.[22]

One of her primary roles in life was to ensure her children acquired the same love of God and reverence for the bible that she had, and had learnt from her own mother. In January 1697 she wrote of her 2-year-old son George, the future Jacobite General:

> George is one of the finest boys that can be; if ye heard him say the prayers it would make you laugh heartily. He takes a book and first he reads then he sings the psalms in his own little fashion and then kneels down and prays for papa and mama and the cat and the rest of his acquaintances.[23]

From Dunkeld Katherine described to the duke how their daughter Susan was repeatedly questioning her:

> ... you would have thought very strong if you had heard her after she asked me who was the first man, the oldest, the wisest, the strongest, the meekest, the patientest and abundance more such queries she asked me how many covenants there were and how many sacraments and from what they were then she asked me how many commands there were ... I was amazed to here her then she told me she would be my master and I should be her scoler.[24]

She was also very proactive in her religion outwith the family home, using all her powers of persuasion and influence on her husband, persistently advising him to promote and encourage the installation of Presbyterian ministers where the post fell vacant. At Falkland in 1691, Katherine wrote to her mother,

> ... thou only knowest what a burden it was to me, the fear I was in that my husband should have obstructed a good minister being settled in this place and now, glory to God that has given me to see him in the main, nay I may say the only instrument of bringing a goodly minister, the Rev Mr. John Forrest to this place.[25]

After her death she left her diary to her husband, calling it her 'treasure', which contained her own reflections on life, death and God's will, and showed how dedicated she was to both her religion and her family. When the second son, William, went off to join the navy, the duke allowed him to copy from this book saying it was, 'the greatest treasure I can give you'.[26] Her sons' lives would without doubt have been heavily influenced by this piety and had she lived, she would have continued to encourage her children to stay committed to the Presbyterian church. Whether she would have succeeded or not is another matter, as the family division over religion was to play a significant role in their future. However, her equally strong political views would also have influenced them and in this her view was in accord with the stance her sons would take.

As Countess of Tullibardine and later Duchess of Atholl, she was her husband's representative in the shire, as he was frequently absent both in Edinburgh and London, but in addition to this she didn't hold back from expressing her own opinion to the him. In fact she gained a reputation for very active involvement, among her family too, as her sister-in-law Elizabeth, the Duchess of Hamilton, wrote to her husband from Kinneil wishing he could join her but, 'your politick self designing sister will prevail to keep you where you are.'[27]

When the Earl of Tullibardine was in London she was his principal source of political intelligence. She had a crucial role to play in drumming up support for his candidate (Murray's brother James) during the 1702 elections and for this she entertained leading people at Huntingtower and fed back information to her husband in London. Her father-in-law, the marquis, pledged his support for Katherine in this, writing that he, 'would goe to my daughter at Huntingtower and doe all I can'.[28] Despite his father and wife's support and best efforts, James Murray failed to win the election and Katherine, very disappointed at the outcome wrote: 'it's neither possible nor fit to tell you particulars here but in short you are most treacherously betrayed by those you most trusted.'[29]

Along with her husband, she was very much against the union and frequently let him know her mind on it: 'I cannot believe … that any English are serious for an union with Scotland on any honourable terms for us.'[30] She had previously voiced similar opinions on English behaviour in the Darien scheme.

Among the documents in the Blair Archives is a poem she wrote entitled 'On the Union'.

> Before the Thistle and the Rose is Twined
> Our Patriots about it thus Divin'd
> Two pots the one of brass ye other of hame
> Were carried by the violence of a streame
> The brasen cry'd come sister joyne my side
> We when continguass shall more safely ride
> I will protect you from ye winde and wave
> And from ye rocke yr brittle fabrick save
> They joyne and doune ye River justling pass
> Till the lame by brasen chattered was
> By this their Union she was more undone
> Then if she had outbraved the storme alone
> Tere's non who breath in Caledonias Aire
> But feel how much this Union did impaire
> Her fabrick: And shall we our scars forgett
> And to our ruine be now more unite
> Unite on such a bottme will is bring
> Under subjection to an English King
> Unite and on such termes we must at once
> Our independence and our King renounce
> Part with our money and our ancient rights
> Turne traitors and be worse than Gibeonites*[31]

Lamentably, Katherine was never to witness what she clearly dreaded.

Sickness and death were ever present in the Murray household, and Katherine had to cope with the emotions of this throughout her life. The death of her first daughter Anne (named after her mother), had a profound effect on her. It's more than likely she suffered post-

---

* (In the Old Testament the Gibeonites tricked Joshua into forming an alliance with them.)

natal depression after this and unfortunately, it was the first of several infant deaths experienced by the family. She also constantly feared and prayed for the health of her husband and children. While staying at Falkland around 1690, Lord Murray suffered a severe form of consumption and his health was in an unstable state for several lengthy periods throughout his life. In 1691 Katherine wrote in her diary:

> Thou knowest I have this day promised if thou wilt be pleased to spare and recover him, to endeavour, through thy strength to live more watchfully and holily … thou has not only allowed of a lawful love to my husband, but commanded me to have it. Therefore it is lawful, and my duty, to pray for him. Spare him O Lord! For Christ's sake, and bless him with a long life in this world, that he may glorify thee in his generation and be an instrument of doing good to the people among whom thou has set him, and be a blessing to his family.[32]

Katherine wasn't immune to sickness herself and, in fact, came very close to dying in November 1696. During a journey to London she stopped at Belford in the North East of England, where she rapidly developed an illness which lasted for twenty days and was so severe her sister Susan, Countess of Dundonald, who was looking after her, feared for her life.[33] The correspondence she sent to her brothers and their mother showed a rapid deterioration in Katherine's condition and increasing concern for her survival. Ultimately Anne, the Dowager Duchess was sent for and arrived in time to see her daughter gradually improve; naturally, this was a very worrying time for the whole family. The illness was later described by the doctors in *The Case of the Countess of Tullibardine*, produced at the request of her husband who had been very alarmed at the severity of it.

> My lady was of a strong healthful body but by frequent miscarrying and great loss of blood her strength has been much weakened and broke and my lady of later years has been subject to stomach pains … and a colic that frequently afflicted her lady ship especially when she was not with child.[34]

Fortunately, on this occasion, however she did recover.

She was very ill once again during her pregnancy of 1700 and Lady Lovat, staying with her parents, wrote expressing the concern of the Murray family:

> My father bids me tell you they are very sorry to hear my Lady Tullibardine has been so extreme ill and wishes for better news of her when my brother James returns. I was extremely sorry when I read your letter that my lady Tullibardine had been so very ill but I hope in God before this she is recovering which I heartily wish and long to hear soon.[35]

Severe sickness during her multiple pregnancies was clearly taking its toll on Katherine's general health and sadly, after a relatively short illness during a visit to her mother at Hamilton in January 1707, she died.

While staying in Edinburgh during debates on the union, the duke had been unaware of how serious his wife's condition was. He expressed great concern and surprise when he was informed of it, writing to her that, 'vexation and trouble has occasioned it, which I beg of you to forebeare since it does you so much hurt.'[36] A few days later he received a letter from the doctor which said she was in danger so he left Edinburgh immediately, at six in the morning, to go to her. Two miles from Hamilton he was met by the doctor who gave him the news that Katherine had died. The duke later wrote:

> I did cast myself on the ground where I doe not remember what I said or did. I was indeed in the height of bitterness and sorrow without any comforter. But the crys and tears of my two sons joining with mine seemed some way satisfying to me that their tender years & affections were sensible of my and their own irreparable loss.[37]

Without the presence of such a strong mother, her sons' lives would inevitably be changed from that moment on. It is difficult to ascertain how much, and what kind of, influence Katherine would have had on her sons' future had she lived, but inevitably her role would have been significant. Given her determined nature, the strong opinions she held throughout her life, and the influence she had in both families, she would not have been passive during the important events the next decade was to bring. Caught among husband and sons it is easy to assume she would have been a reconciling factor and tried to heal the rifts between them; however, she didn't manage this with her eldest son, quite the opposite, so would she have had more success with the others? Her commitment to the Presbyterian church was very strong, but she was also very vocal in her anti-Union stance and as a loyal sister and member of the Hamilton family it is improbable to think she would have quietly accepted the death of her eldest brother, the Duke of Hamilton and the subsequent treatment of one of the protagonists.

Chapter 6

Hamilton and Nairne Families

Bereft after the death of his wife, the duke soon acknowledged a need for advice and support on his children's upbringing and in this, as well as in political issues, he regularly consulted Katherine's mother Anne, the Dowager Duchess of Hamilton.

Lady Anne Hamilton became duchess after the death of her uncle William in 1651. Her father James, 1st Duke of Hamilton, a supporter of Charles I, had been executed in 1649 leaving his titles and estates to his brother William. He had requested his brother be a father to his two daughters and prevent them from being forced to marry against their will. However, two years later William also died from wounds received at the Battle of Worcester fighting for Charles II. William had no sons but had such a high opinion of his niece Anne, that he claimed, 'if [I] had had forty sons [I] rather wished the inheritance to Anne than [I] would to any of them.'[1] Anne therefore became the 3rd Duchess of Hamilton in her own right but was unable to claim her entitlement to the estates as they had been confiscated and handed over to officers in Cromwell's army. Instead she lived for a while in Brodick, Arran, but then returned to the Hamilton area. Tradition has it that she was so impoverished during this time that she relied on a domestic servant spinning wool to provide for her, and though this may be a myth, or at least an exaggeration of the facts, she did gift a substantial piece of land to a domestic servant in later years.

Anne married William Douglas, Earl of Selkirk, in 1656; although a Roman Catholic, he converted to the Presbyterian church and, at Anne's request, was made Duke of Hamilton in his lifetime. With the restoration of Charles II in 1660 she took possession of her father's estates, but also inherited the huge family debts associated with them. However, with her husband's assistance and the repayment of a £25,000 loan made by Anne's father to the monarch, she became solvent again and began the rebuilding of their estate in the 1670s. This vast rebuild included work at Kinneil and Crawford Castle, but by far the most extravagant was the project at Hamilton Palace which would eventually become the largest private residence in Europe. After such a turbulent recent past, the Hamiltons needed to enforce the prestige and pedigree of their family, and this was a very effective way of doing it.

In his three-volume travel book *A tour thro' the whole island of Great Britain, divided into circuits or journies* published between 1724 and 1727, Daniel Defoe described Hamilton Palace:

> The front is very magnificent indeed, all of white freestone, with regular ornaments according to the rules of art: The wings are very deep, and when the other wings come to be added, if ever that shall be, the two sides of the house will then be like two large fronts rather than wings; not unlike Beddington House, near Croydon in Surrey, only much larger … The apartments are very noble, and fit rather for the court of a prince than the palace or house of a subject; the pictures, the furniture, and the decoration of every thing is not to be describ'd, but by saying that every thing is exquisitely fine and suitable to the genius of the great possessors.[2]

Scotland was experiencing a significant building boom at this time and no doubt knowledge gained from this, and the enthusiasm shown by her parents, would have had an impact on the duke and duchess' daughter Katherine, whose home at Huntingtower would undergo significant renovations as part of her marriage agreement.

Throughout her life Anne was in regular contact with her large family, dispensing advice and being consulted on many issues in family matters and the wider world, and was therefore actively involved in many crucial events. The image created from her correspondence is one of Anne being a highly respected and influential matriarch who was kept informed politically and socially on many levels by a variety of people, and who used this power to help her family whenever she could. Her position in society meant she was looked up to by many of her peers and was regarded as a good indicator of social norms. She invested heavily in the Darien scheme, for example, and of the massacre at Glencoe she wrote to Katherine in 1700: 'I think the murder at Glencoe is a crying sin that aught publickly to be mourned for.'[3] She was, however, cautious and astute enough to know that she should be careful in what she wrote. She advised her daughter to burn her letters after reading them and suggested a numbering system to ensure they both knew they had received what was sent.[4] In later years she was unable to write herself due to ill health; gout and arthritis meant she couldn't hold a pen and she didn't always trust the people who transcribed for her, which must have restricted her correspondence significantly.

In later life, due to the death of Anne's children James, Katherine and Basil, she had many of her grandchildren stay with her in Hamilton, for different periods of their lives; a situation she couldn't have foreseen, but took on despite suffering ill health. She welcomed having the grandchildren, though admitted struggling at times. Locally she was known as 'the good duchess Anne', and was respected and admired by her tenants and the wider district. An anecdote in her daughter's diary tells of an incident at the celebration of the Lord's Supper when Anne stepped up to the table at the same time as another plain, aged member, who then stepped aside to give her precedence. The duchess, however, was unwilling to receive such marks of attention and respect in the church and said, 'step forward honest woman there is no distinction of ranks here.'[5] It was this type of incident as well as her piety and commitment to Presbyterianism which had such an effect on Katherine and influenced her in her own way of life.

Anne's relationship with her son-in-law, John Murray, was very strong, being one of mutual respect and understanding, and contrasted starkly with that of her own eldest son James, Duke of Hamilton. Their relationship was strained and tense, on many occasions pushing Anne and William's (his father), patience to its limit. In 1703 after the death of Murray's mother, Anne offered him advice on how to cope, informing her daughter of this she wrote: 'I have a son will not be so grieved for me.'[6]

After the sudden death of his wife in 1707, Anne provided a great deal support to the duke, both emotional and practical. The frequent correspondence between them showed his high regard and deference to her. In one he writes: 'I shall continue my most ardent prayers for your Grace so long as I live, to preserve you for the good of your family and your relations who will follow your good advice which I have always endeavoured to do.'[7] Two of his daughters, Susan and Katherine, went to live with her for some time, and his sons frequently spent time there too. She was consulted for her opinions repeatedly and it was Anne he turned to for advice and help when his sons began to dissent. Equally, it was to her and their uncles (Anne's sons) that the boys would turn when they needed the assistance they weren't getting from their father. After Katherine's death, her brothers became significantly involved in their nephews' welfare and often wrote to Anne of how the duke's sons were getting on. They also made well-intentioned suggestions of what she should advise Atholl to do, as both the Earl of Selkirk and Earl of Orkney became increasingly critical of his methods.

The Hamilton influence on the Murray family wasn't limited to Anne of course; her children – aunts and uncles to the Murray brothers' inevitably had a considerable impact on their lives. Charles, Earl of Selkirk, was the third son of the Duke and Duchess of Hamilton; an early supporter of King William, he was appointed one of the Lords of the Bedchamber, an office he held under Queen Anne and George's I & II. In 1696 he was appointed Lord Clerk Register of Scotland and in 1713 one of the sixteen chosen representatives of the Scottish Peerage.

George, Earl of Orkney, the Hamilton's fifth son, had a very successful military career, distinguishing himself fighting for William in Ireland, including the Battle of the Boyne, and was made Brigadier General. His services were rewarded by his being made a peer in Scotland and in 1702 was promoted to major general, then in 1703 to lieutenant general, as well as a Knight of the Thistle. He took part in all the major battles of the Nine Years War, serving under the Duke of Marlborough, and contributed to the victories of Blenheim, Ramilies, Oudenard and Malplaquet. In 1714 he was appointed gentleman extraordinary of the bedchamber to George I and was the first British Army officer to be promoted to the rank of field marshal.

Both these men had great affection for their nephews, but were also fair and un-blinkered in their opinions. They didn't consider their nephews faultless, and in Lord George's case in particular they were quite critical. Their main censure, though, was for the Duke of Atholl himself. While respectful of his status, and the fact that he was their sister's husband, they could at times be quite scathing and unsympathetic, especially when it came to finances. However, when called on for help during the events of the 1715 Rising and its aftermath, they did all they could to assist their nephews and the duke.

The Hamilton's eldest son James, who became the 4th Duke, no doubt also had a significant influence his nephews' lives, as he was a major political player in royal court and parliamentary politics, spending much of his time in London. The biggest effect this duke had on the Murray brothers, however, was the manner and timing of his death. Poised to embark on a royal diplomatic trip to France, he instead agreed to meet his long-time adversary Lord Mohun in Hyde Park, London, for a duel; both were killed. Their quarrel had been over the inheritance of the Macclesfield Estate; the 4th Earl had died without heirs in 1702 and left the inheritance to Mohun, who had been married to a granddaughter of the 1st Earl, but Hamilton claimed his wife – who was also a granddaughter – had the better claim. Due to their lifestyles both men had considerable debts and needed the money, but they were also of opposing parties in parliament.

Duelling, or calling someone out, crops up frequently in this period. There are a surprising number of instances of nobles choosing to take this course of action to settle disputes, especially considering it was illegal – not only for the duellists themselves, but also for their seconds. The Duke of Atholl, in his earlier years, challenged Lord Breadalbane, but friends persuaded him not to go through with it. Katherine was spared the grief of the death of her eldest son but had she lived, she would no doubt have been horrified to discover that the marquis had threatened the Prince of Orange with a duel which was to take place after the next military engagement.[8] On some occasions the duellists were political allies. For example, demonstrating the lack of cohesion among the Hanoverian forces, in February 1716, the leading officers from the Battle of Preston, Generals Wills and Carpenter, were reported to have challenged each other.[9] Higher up the Hanoverian military scale there was gossip of a challenge being made by the Duke of Argyll to General Cadogan, who had been sent to replace him in Scotland.[10]

Inevitably, the Hamilton family and their relatives reacted with astonishment when the news reached them of the Duke of Hamilton's death. The Earl of Panmure wrote to Atholl:

> I cannot express the grief both my wife and I are in for the Duke of Hamilton's death it is indeed ane exceedingly great loss to his relations and to the wholl nation in general. I am afraid that this may very much endanger My lady Duchess his mother's health, we sent a footman to Hamilton on Monday to enquire how she is but he is not yet returned.[11]

A letter to His Grace in the Blair Archives expressed the shock felt by many: 'The melancholy account of his grace the Duke of Hamiltons tragicall death would undoubtedly be very worrying to your Grace especially the way and manner of it. That one of his quality and station should dye in the hands of such Barbarous Ruffians.'[12]

It was Lord Mohn's second, George MacCartney, who was accused, probably incorrectly, of dealing the fatal blow to Hamilton. Both families were outraged and sought redress by a just punishment for him. Atholl went to London to pay his respects to the widowed Duchess of Hamilton and wait on the queen who, he said, expressed regret at the 'great loss' of the Duke of Hamilton and reported: 'she would use her utmost endeavours to have McCartney arrested when it could be known where he was.'[13]

Atholl also organised a petition to the queen calling for MacCartney to be apprehended and charged.

> We being deeply affected with the barbarous and execsable murder committed upon James Duke of Hamilton and Duke of Brandon by George MacKarntey and that as the publik in general

so we in particular have sustained an expresable loss by the death of so worthy and great a man and good patriot we give your majesty our most humble thanks for the care your majesty has taken in emitting your Royal proclamation for apprehending the said George MacKartney And we humby entreat your majesty be grievously pleased to give such further orders and direction as in your Royal wisdom shall be thought fit for apprehending George Mackartney wherever he shall be found in any part of your Majesties dominions. As al that your majesty may be greviously pleased to give orders to your ministers in soverign kingdoms and states to demand the said George Mackartney wherever he shall be discovered that he may be sent to Britain in order to be brought to justice.[14]

This petition had fifty signatories including Atholl, Mar, Breadalbane, Forbes, Aberdeen, Leven and Kilmarnock.

A proclamation from the queen was issued 24 November 1712 which stated:

… that if any person or persons after the issuing of the Our Royal Proclamation shall directly or indirectly conceal, harbour keep or maintain the said George MacCartney or shall be aiding or assisting to hi in making his escape or prevent his being taken or arrested, such person or persons so offending shall be prosecuted for the same with the utmost severity for the Law.[15]

MacCartney was forced into exile, but after two years abroad (and the death of Queen Anne) he returned to face trial; convicted only as an accessory, he was excused and, as a favourite of George I, was later given several enviable, lucrative posts in the army. This was met with great resentment by the Hamilton and Murray families and wasn't something they were prepared to forget or reconcile themselves to without further repercussions.

A fourth uncle whose untimely death would also have had a huge impact on his nephews was Lord Basil Hamilton. In contrast to his flamboyant, rebellious and unpredictable brother James, Basil was the dependable, reliable, stay-at-home sibling both Katherine and many others turned to for advice and assistance. While her other brothers had left the family home in Hamilton to advance their careers elsewhere, Basil had stayed in the area to help his mother with the estate. He was highly respected by many in all levels of society, described in Douglas' Peerage as, 'a young man of distinguished abilities, great spirit and an amiable disposition'. It was Basil who had given John Murray moral support and guidance during his trial against Lord Balnagoun as well as keeping the family up to date on its progress, and it was Basil who helped to reconcile Murray and his father, the marquis, in a dispute in 1700. This was acknowledged by the marquis who thanked Basil for the efforts he had made to try and 'establish a lasting friendship such as ought to be betwixt us'.[16]

More significantly, Basil had played a vital role in the aftermath of the debacle that was the Darien expedition when he was sent as a representative to plead to King William on behalf of some passengers who had been taken prisoner. Lord Basil had been an enthusiastic supporter of the enterprise since its inception in 1695 when an Act was passed in the Scottish Parliament establishing a Company of Scotland Trading to Africa and the Indies. The idea had come from William Paterson a founder of the Bank of England in 1694. He had proposed a Scottish colony in Central America at Darien, now part of Panama, which would be crucial to trade coming across the Pacific and where cargoes from the East Indies and Asia could exchange goods. Unfortunately, Paterson had never actually been to Darien.

The company was to be entirely financed by public subscription and several Hamilton family members invested, including Basil himself and his mother the duchess, who was one of the first to put her name down in order to encourage others. By August of 1696, £400,000 had been raised in Scotland from all sections of society, almost half the country's available capital, but English investors had withdrawn fearing the monopoly of the East India Company would be broken by the scheme. The king had also turned against the idea as it interfered, as ever, with his war plans and his needing to be on good terms with Spain. Scottish investors, however, remained hopeful and committed to the project. The first expedition departed in 1698, with great promise, but met with repeated setbacks.

The king had instructed his colonies not to deal with the company, the land was unsuitable, and the colonists were affected badly by tropical diseases, inadequate supplies and internal feuding. By July 1699 it was abandoned. Unaware of this disaster, a second expedition was prepared in Scotland which Lord Basil enthusiastically assisted. He visited Greenock himself, reporting to his brother the Duke of Hamilton that the ships were just waiting for a fair wind before they could leave. To his brother-in-law, Tullibardine, he wrote:

> thers about 1500 as good men as ever we seen, and of them I believe 200 gentlemen. We have not an ill man to look to there being such abundance to choose of and many that are very willing to goe we can't take them at this time.[17]

But shortly after their departure word began to arrive of the failure of the first expedition. Basil wrote to Tullibardine that they were very perplexed by the confirmed surprising account of their colony's desertion in Darien.[18] However, when these initial reports were confirmed later Basil was clearly devastated.

> It is not to be expressed the melancholy condition I am in; I'm touched to the very soul and ashamed to be seen. We shall appear despicable to the world; it seems God Almighty sees it not time yett to deliver us from our misery butt to tryst us with affliction on the back of affliction.[19]

When news reached the directors of the company that a group of colonists had been taken prisoner by the Spanish, several, including the Earl of Panmure and Marquis of Tweedale, agreed that Lord Basil was the ideal candidate to go to London and plead their case to the king: 'no one would be more suitable than Lord Basil.'[20] He went to London with the support of everyone concerned. King William, however, refused to see him. After a further petition by the directors through the Lord Chancellor, an audience was finally agreed which was to take place in the council chamber. William forgot the appointment and proceeded to pass into another chamber when Lord Basil placed himself in front of the king and declared he had a right to be heard. William eventually did agree and gave an order to apply to Spain for their release, but he had been heard to say: 'This young man is too bold, if any man can be too bold in his country's cause.'[21]

In 1701, while escorting his brother Lord Selkirk from Baldoon in Galloway back to Hamilton, the group were crossing the River Minnick when Lord Basil noticed one of the young servants' horse had fallen, throwing the servant off. Basil rode back into the water to save him. Unable to do so on horseback, he dismounted to follow the boy on foot, but fell into the river himself and was carried away. His body was found three-quarters-of-an-hour later about a mile further down the river, he was 30 years old and left a young pregnant wife and children. Needless to say, his family and friends were heartbroken. Had Lord Basil survived, without doubt he would have been instrumental in helping negotiate the future troubles of the various members of his family. He had already been involved in talks concerning his brother the Duke of Hamilton's marriage settlement, so perhaps could have prevented the escalation of that issue, and he had reconciled one Murray father-and-son relationship, so could well have helped resolve future ones. It is fair to say his early loss was particularly detrimental to the family.

His wife Mary gave birth a few months later. Tullibardine wrote, 'My wife is still at Hamilton where she stays till Lady Mary Hamilton is brought to bed which is the least duty we owe to the wife of the best of men and friends- I shall not enter on so sad a subject here.'[22] In 1704 Katherine gave birth to a son, her last child and named him Basil.

On the Universally Lamented Death of the Right Honourable Lord Basil Hamilton, brother to his Grace the Duke of Hamilton. (Being a short hit of his heroic life and fatal death) who died August 1701.

> Ah! How all elements conspire with Death,
> To stifle at it's pleasure human breath!

The very water here at its command,
Destroys a Peer and Pillar of this land;
Basil, who was descended from that lne,
where brightest rays of royaltie do shine,
Who next the Duke, was Phoenix of his name
And house, which everywhere diffuse their fame
Whose personage was so symmetrical,
All justly him, his father's image call,
And in whose stately fabrick lodged was
A soul, which other souls did far surpass:
A soul, consults the good of Caledon,
As if in both, were not two souls but one.
A soul, through his short course of life was free
From swearing, drunkeness and leacherie.
And treacherie and all other crimes
Which are the horrid scandal of these times.
With sublime sence, and courage he withstood
Whatever did oppose the publick good,
And he his charitie did so extend
All Caledonia will him still commend,
As their thrice worthie patriot and friend,
Ah! fatal instance of his charitie!
To save a menial servant he did die.
Ah! that the cruel fates would not allow
What to that most heroic deed was due!
Here his attempt the fates did render vain,
As they did those of his for Darien.

Scottish Elegaic Verses edited by James Maidment

In addition to the Hamiltons, John Murray's brother William and his wife Margaret Nairne were also a major influence in the Murray brothers' upbringing; living at the House of Nairne, near Letham, meant they were quite local and within reach of Dunkeld, Huntingtower and Blair. However, theirs was a very different household to that of the Murrays and Hamiltons – they were Episcopalian and committed Jacobites.

Margaret, Lady Nairne, was the daughter and heiress of Robert, first Lord Nairne and contractually obliged to marry a Murray in order to keep her title. She was at first betrothed to John Murray's brother George, but due to his ill health she married instead the younger brother William who was to share her Jacobite sympathies. He took the surname Nairne at their marriage in 1690 and inherited the title. Their children were also strong Jacobite supporters; their eldest son, John, was captured with his father in 1715 and also fought at Culloden, as did a second son Robert. Their daughter Margaret married William Drummond, 4th Viscount Strathallan, who was killed at Culloden; Amelia married Laurence Oliphant of Gask, who fought for the Jacobites in the 1745 rising; Marjory married Duncan Robertson of Struan and endured a long exile with him; Catherine married her cousin, William Murray, 3rd Earl of Dunmore, again a Jacobite in 1745. Charlotte, who married John Robertson of Lude, was reported to have bullied her tenants into joining the Jacobite army in the 45 by threatening to burn their homes down if they didn't. Louisa married the Jacobite Graeme of Orchill. The only Whig of the family was James, whom their mother referred to as her 'lost sheep'.[23]

The Nairnes were in regular contact with the Murrays and included in many of their domestic affairs. Margaret, for example, was at Huntingtower when Lady Katherine gave birth in 1702. On at least two occasions Lord Nairne took over at Huntingtower when his brother went to London, keeping an eye on his interests there. They also became embroiled in several unexpected and anxious family events, helping to track down Johny when he disappeared from home in 1704 and persuading him to return:

> I can't possibly describe the trouble we are both in upon your Grace's account, the young gentleman's and most of all for my lady Duchess, whom I pray God this incident mayn't harm. I would have gone just now to waited on her Grace, but perhaps you have not yet told her and then my coming to Dunkeld so much sooner then I writt to her yesterday might surprize her.[24]

The duchess, at this time, was pregnant. On a second occasion it was at their house that the Murrays' son George sought sanctuary, when he too ran away from school.

Lord Nairne suffered frequently through ill health and this probably contributed to William's wife Margaret being a prolific correspondent on his behalf as well as her own, and came to have the most significant influence on her husband's nephews. She was a strong character who clearly developed a genuine interest in the politics and the future of her country. Until Katherine's death in 1707, both the Duke and Duchess of Atholl were on close terms with Margaret; they wrote to each other frequently and she was often consulted on a variety of matters including the health and welfare of the children, as well as current affairs, and even assisted in the drawings of designs for new building projects.[25] A strong bond of sisterly friendship existed between Margaret and Katherine, especially in domestic matters, despite their differences in religion, and for much of the time the families enjoyed a healthy relationship. They all three, for example, saw the lighter side to the marquis and his wife choosing a date for Lady Lovat's daughter's wedding. Margaret wrote:

> I could not but laugh when I read that part of your Lordships letter wherein you say Lady Lovat named four weeks the end of which her daughter would be satisfied to marry. I find they carefully shun telling you they will not have her to wed in lent perhaps for fear you should think them half papists.[26]

In addition to her friendship with Katherine, Margaret had a close relationship with Katherine's sister, Margaret Maule the Countess of Panmure, the Murray brothers' aunt, with whom she had more in common – both in politics and religion. The more radical opinions expressed in these letters increased after Katherine's death when Lady Nairne's own attitude and allegiances became more resolute. On 8 March 1708 a warrant had been issued for the arrest of Lord Nairne for acting as an intermediary between France and Scotland during the 1707 preparation of a French invasion and Scottish rising. He was taken as a prisoner to London, where his wife travelled to plead for his release.

It was around this time her bonhomie with the Duke of Atholl began to deteriorate. Perhaps Atholl felt the association with his obviously Jacobite brother was too risky, but the death of his wife had also deprived Margaret of a strong connection with the duke, and it was clear her own inclinations were taking her towards an increased involvement in politics that didn't conform with his. Margaret was not pleased when the duke married Mary Ross, a Presbyterian from a loyal Hanoverian family, in 1710, because she would clearly never be able to foster the same relationship with this new wife as she'd had with Katherine. The disapproval of Mary Ross was to change after the 1715 rebellion, however, when Duchess Mary was asked by several Murray relations to use her influence help their Jacobite relatives in prison.

During the 1715 rebellion Margaret made a conscious decision to support the Jacobites, along with her husband and son, and was in communication with the Earl of Mar, who praised her commitment, wishing all men under his command had the spirit of Lady Nairne.[27] The Duke of Atholl, on the other hand, later regretted the amount of influence Margaret had had during his sons' upbringing and wrote to his son James in June 1716, after the rebellion: 'I hope you have as little to do with my Lady Nairne as possible for there cannot be a worse woman. I impute the ruine of my three sons to her artifices.'[28]

Chapter 7

Johny

John and Katherine's eldest son was born 6 May 1684 at Kinneil house, a property of the Hamilton's on the outskirts of Bo'ness. Frequently referred to as Johny or Johnnie in early family letters he was, as his father had been, the heir to the family titles and estates and the prospect of this future inheritance was inevitably reflected in the manner of his upbringing. All decisions regarding his education, career and possible marriage were made by his parents to enhance the family name and position in society. Unfortunately for them, however, he was far from compliant and had a strong independent streak which led to frequent clashes with his parents and many exasperated letters between them, as well as pleas from his parents to other relatives, to talk some sense into him. The lives of his younger brothers, William and George, are well recorded in Scottish history but this eldest brother is rarely mentioned. His death and the drama of it at the young age of 25, however, would without doubt have had a huge impact on the younger brothers, who were brought up expecting him to become the head of the family and therefore have a significant influence over their own lives.

Johny was the couple's eldest child; a second, Anne, died at 14 months of age, a third, Mary, born in 1686 died aged 2, and a fourth, Amelia, also died aged 2, which no doubt meant that he was particularly precious to them. Throughout his life, while he frequently caused his parents great anxiety, he was very popular and loved by the many members of the Murray and Hamilton families, who all showed genuine affection and fondness for him, he was even favoured by royalty. In comparison to his younger siblings he was at times indulged in his wishes and had more success at getting his own way, but he also carried the burden of higher expectations from his parents. It was perhaps his response to this indulgence which set the pattern for their father's future attitude to his other sons, as it made the duke cautious not to repeat the mistake.

In July 1693 Lord Murray, aged 9, accompanied his father to London where they lived briefly at a house in Pall Mall, after which they moved to St James Street where they were later joined by Katherine. He then went to a school in Hackney which was kept by a Frenchman, Monsieur Leniere, and where he spent over two years until he was put to another school in London in 1696. There, an agreement between the schoolmaster, Mr Cappell, and Katherine was made for his board and education: she paid £34 by quarterly payments plus 'forty shillings beside for fire and one silver porrenger and silver spoon and three pounds sterling for entrance.'[1] By 1699 he had returned to Scotland as his father, keenly aware of his inheritance and future responsibilities, wanted him to go to the 'highlands to lairne Irish'.[2] There he stayed for a while with Mr Munro Murray, the minister of Logierait living in Balnamuir.[3]

By 1701 he had his own governor at Huntingtower, Thomas Fleming, who was clearly unimpressed with Johny's attitude to study and wrote to his father:

> I'm sorry that I am still forced by my Lord Murrays conduct to complain of him, he continues to be as disrespectful and disobedient as ever and has been more lasie and more idle this last week than the week before … as for his reading he read some latine, Irish and french on Munday last, but Tuesday, Wednesday and Thursday he did not read one word of ane thing or other except a chapter in the bible … his answers when desired to do any thing are ordinarily I will not! When I think fit! When it pleaseth me … my Lady Susan and all the masters are in good health.

As a post script he adds, 'it was again within a quarter of nine before my Lord rose this morning and but just now dressed tho it be passed ten a clock.'[4] Johny was 16 years old at this point and this attitude will come as no surprise to most parents of teenagers today.

Poor performance at their studies becomes a common theme among the boys of the Murray family. At the end of one of the duke's letters to Johny he wrote, 'your writing is so bad I have difficulty to read your letters.'[5] In hindsight it is easy to identify that this lack of academic ability probably played a significant role in leading some of the brothers to follow careers their parents didn't approve of. However, at their young age it is hardly surprising the onerous task of estate management and dutiful service didn't seem to appeal to any of them. Ultimately, they were all to choose a military life rather than the responsibilities of the estate and gaining political power at court.

Despite his reluctance, however Johny's parents were determined he had a role to play in ensuring that the family maintained its position in the wider political world, and they continued to pursue further education and the experiences they thought he needed to equip him for this future. With this in mind, in 1702 he accompanied his father to London again. Katherine charged her husband with keeping a strict eye on him and advised: 'I hope he'll remember to keep good company and be much with you and follow your advice and mind you often to have a cair of your health. I recommended to him to red much in the proverbs of Solomon where he'll have the best advice given him.'[6] In further letters she sent her blessings to Johny, 'who I pray God keepe from evil company.[7]

Later that year he returned to Perthshire to assist his mother during the local elections, working hard at what proved to be a fruitless task, but his efforts were admired by Katherine who was delighted to be able to report to his father that he had been so useful:

I have undertaken to yr son to make his excuses for not writing to you, he has not indeed been idle since he came here and I must in the first place tell you I am most extremely well pleased with him and am rejoiced to see with what concernedness and prudence and diligence he has gone about what you recommended to him in his Uncles affair so let this comfort you in the disappointment of it.[8]

Unfortunately, he blotted his copy book shortly after this by having an extended stay at his uncle's house when his mother had expected his help at their home at Huntingtower. She clearly had strict words with him about it and in a particularly emotional letter wrote to her husband:

> I have just gotten the enclosed from my Lady Dunmore which how it has vexed me and what a passion it put me into I shall not here say I pray God forgive me ... to be displeased with what your son has done and what your brother and Lady Dunmore part has been I think you have good reason for, it's very hard since your friends will not help you that they should take away your son also ... I must say they have been very wrong to keep your son when he told you what necessity there was for his coming and I think you should let my Lady Dunmore know so much that you take it not well, it is a pretty thing indeed that she would make her journey of more consequence than the elections.[9]

In early 1703 Johny was back in London again but had returned to Scotland by May, as according to his father,

> ... he does no good here but follows his own irregular appetites. I cannot so much as prevaile with him to come home before 10 o'clock at night which he thinks is a hard imposition, he has been speaking of going to see the summer campaign in Flanders which I should not think very unreasonable if he were one could be trusted, for how will he obey our commands at a distance when he will not obey both lawful and reasonable ones at home.[10]

At the end of June, however, Lord Murray had got his wish and was sent to the Netherlands with his governor Thomas Fleming. He had pleaded with his father to let him go to see the campaign, to satisfy his curiosity and extend his education and, despite great unwillingness and a distinct lack of funds, his father had agreed.

The campaigning was part of the Wars of the Spanish Succession, a global conflict which included colonial possessions in the Americas and West Indies. The question of who would inherit the Spanish throne had dominated the European political scene for years as King

Carlos II had been mentally and physically challenged from birth and though married twice, had produced no heir. Leading rival claimants had attempted to agree on a partition of the Spanish Kingdom before his death, but this failed. When Charles died in 1700 he named Philip, Duke of Anjou, as his successor to the entire Spanish kingdom and Philip naturally received the support of his grandfather, Louis XIV of France. The prospect of a potential unification of these two countries and the subsequent shift of balance of power worldwide, united primarily the countries of England, the Netherlands, Austria and Prussia in the Grand Alliance against France and Spain in 1701, and war was declared in 1702. Campaigning took place from April to October with the British forces being led by the Duke of Marlborough who was a personal acquaintance of the Duke of Atholl and his family.

With many members of his immediate family (both Murray and Hamilton) involved in the campaigns, the restless Lord Murray, keen to escape the strict censure of his parents, was eager to be allowed to witness what was happening first hand. After an initial reluctance, his father gave in and used the opportunity to propose a marriage alliance between his son and the Duke of Marlborough's daughter Mary Churchill, sending a letter to Marlborough with his son suggesting this. Although the idea was well received by the Duchess of Marlborough, a marriage never took place.[11]

From the Hague in July 1703 John wrote to his mother asking her to intercede on his behalf by requesting more money from his father. As the issue doesn't come up again during his stay it's fair to assume he got the extra funds he required. Perhaps this was due to his new status as, with his father's elevation to duke, he had now become the Marquis of Tullibardine. In October he spent some time with the army reaching Limburg after its surrender and staying ultimately at Utrecht. By November he again returned to London to spend time with his father. However, far from settling down to his new role, there were an increasing number of incidents of youthful exuberance and high spirits which weren't in keeping with the image his parents were trying to foster.

Accompanying his father in London he was no doubt under strict instructions to live up to his new title and responsibilities. Among other roles he had the job of providing regular communication to his family in Scotland which included keeping them up to date with information on 'the Scotch plot', in which the duke had been framed as a principal participant. However, Katherine wasn't impressed with her son's lack of efficiency and reprimanded him for not being more useful to his father. His reply was a lengthy letter defending himself, claiming he had written more than enough letters to keep his relations up to date:

> I believe your Grace has, if they have not miscarried, a good number of my letters since I came to London and I have told in them all that I know of occurances there and what my Lord bid me which even might have been done fewer letters and I believe there are several in Scotland understand much of this plot by my writing such accounts of it as I could.

This vindication of his activities was quickly followed by the announcement of his future intentions:

> I have been desiring of my Lord that he would dispose of me for a year or two in traveling and being in some place wholely employed in reading or other improvements that I am not capable at this age rather than take me now to Scotland which he seems inclined to do. What I have proposed is by far my inclination it is what I hope just and reasonable because it is that a desire to improve myself.

He explained he had discussed these with his uncle, Lord Orkney (the duchess' brother), a possible diplomatic tactic hoping to win his mother over. Lord Orkney at this time was commander of a regiment fighting in the Netherlands:

> My Lord Orkney proposes 600 stirling for my being abroad a year which having great management of myself I should keep within bounds of. So I have layed before your Grace all that I desire

and for what reasons and having not more to say I shall prepare myself all I can to hear patiently whatever happens.[12]

He then pleaded for her help in having these wishes accepted by his father.

From the tone of this letter he seemed very optimistic of a positive outcome to his request so it's highly unlikely he anticipated the reply he got, which was an emphatic 'no':

> As to what you propose of your going abroad again I really could hardly believe my owne eyes when I red it and it seems you have forgote on what terms my Lord condesended to your going when you went last for in my hearing you said if he would but alow your going to see the last campaign you would desire no more and he would then have fully exonered himself as to your education and satisfying your curiosity.[13]

In her opinion he had had more spent on his education than most people already, which had only increased his curiosity rather than satisfy it. She also wasn't particularly happy that he was taking advice about how much to live on from people who were unaware of their financial circumstances and that it was time he took more interest in the affairs the nation and particularly that of his family:

> I know at least I hope so when you consider calmly on it and lay by your little follys of youth you'll be of your fathers minde and mine which in the end you'll find your advantage all manner of ways and that God may bless you and give you direction and conduct and keep you from all the temptations you are liable to is the hearty prayer of your most affectionate mother.[14]

However, even before he received this reply the marquis had been forced to write again to his mother to excuse a more recent incident of which he was concerned she would hear – that he had made a challenge to Lord Stairs, the news of which had already reached the ears of the queen. In what was to become a typically defensive letter he wrote: 'perhaps your Grace may hear something about my Ld Stairs and me, and lest you have not a right account I shall tell how it was.'[15] He described how he had wanted to speak plainly to Lord Stairs, who had accused his father of being in the plot against the queen, and had written a note to him asking for a meeting; the 57-year-old Lord Stairs had taken fright at this because he had thought it was a challenge to a duel. Queen Anne had been informed and had sent the chancellor to make them both swear nothing would happen. The marquis, who claimed he had never intended a duel at all, had made sure the queen knew this and felt sure she was satisfied with his explanation. There's no record of Katherine's response to this, but it doesn't take much imagination to picture the scene on her receipt of this news.

1704 was a significant year in the campaigning in Europe as the Duke of Marlborough joined by Prince Eugene of Savoy gained a resounding victory in August at Blenheim. Atholl received a report by Lord Orkney,

> I am hardly able to give you an account of the great victory we gained yesterday I am so weary. I bless God I have no wounds tho my horse was shot under me. Wee marched yesterday by break of day to attack the enemy in camp. The fight continued from morning till dark at night and ended very happily. It is impossible to tell you now all the circumstances of this battle. It is the greatest that has been fought these 50 years and if it has cost us dear the enemie has pay'd well for it.[16]

It is not unreasonable to assume that the young marquis was frustrated at not being involved in this and felt trapped at home, the expectations of his family burdening him with a role he didn't want. Perhaps this explains why, while staying at Dunkeld with his mother in November 1704, he ran away. From later letters, we can infer that on this particular occasion there was a heated discussion at some point, which more than likely involved money, during which he upset his mother and stormed out of the house.

From his parents' point of view, this was a time of uncertainty and concern within both the Murray and Hamilton households. The duke had been replaced as Lord Privy Seal and was pursuing payment of his salaries and expenses to pay off mounting debts which were causing increasing tension between the family members. The duchess was again heavily pregnant and feeling unwell with it, and a cousin and friend of the marquis', who had gone to Holland as a colonel in George MacArtney's Regiment of Scot Foot, had died. From his parents' point of view, Johny's desire to go abroad again was unreasonable and badly timed. They had already given in to this request, he had had his spell abroad and now they wanted him to stay at home to fulfil the role required of the heir. They didn't have the money to fund another trip abroad and the death of Lord Fincastle, the cousin in Holland, no doubt highlighted the ever-present fear of danger while abroad.

Relatives and friends were immediately called upon to stop Johny from doing anything too rash; before he got far he was overtaken by his uncle, Lord Nairne, who persuaded him to go to Dupplin to cool off before returning to Dunkeld. Initially Johny wanted to go abroad, but he acknowledged that what he had done was unreasonable and, though he was concerned about returning home, was prepared to go back in the company of his uncles. The duke's private secretary, Lesley, wrote that he was showing signs of remorse as, 'my lord Marquis does resent the fears he is in of the danger he may have occasioned his mother, my Lady Duchess, considering her Grace's condition.'[17] Fortunately, the duchess did give birth successfully in December.

From this episode on, however, Katherine seems regularly to despair of her eldest son and the influence others are having on him. She confided to her mother that,

> ... my son's ... whos ways I shall owned to your Grace is very grievous to us what is the ground of my sister P. commending him so much is far from recommending him to us for its being a Jacobit and violent episcopal that makes her think so well of him.[18]

In Katherine's opinion her son thought he knew better than his parents (plus ça change) and he needed to be put back on track by spending more time with his grandmother, including, for example, accompanying her when she travelled, as this would be a more suitable way for him to pass his time. She had a double motive for this approach as Katherine had also appealed to her mother to talk some sense into him, believing she would be able to make a better impression on him. Initially the Dowager Duchess was unsure what help she could be, but following a brief stay by the marquis at Hamilton, she wrote that she had talked a good while with him, intended to return to the subjects they had spoken of, and in her opinion, 'in general he speaks very descretly the Lord make him a comfortable son to his father and you and then he will be a blessing to the family.'[19]

As he seemed to do with most of his relations, Johny made a great impression on the Dowager Duchess, who by the end of the visit was writing that, 'he is so obliging that everybody loves him. I have given him the best advice I could ... to stay home and be as observing of his father and you as was possible as was both his duty and interest.'[20] She also suggest they look for a suitable marriage for him and seemed very hopeful of his future. A second marriage suggestion had been made in April 1704 with Lady Henrietta Stanley, daughter of the Earl of Derby, but it never progressed and in fact the marquis never married.

Despite this positive opinion and promising outlook, by the end of 1705 a total breakdown in the parent and son relationship had occurred; Johny had turned up at the Hague requesting a company in the army from the Duke of Marlborough, while his parents were under the impression he was there continuing his studies. Both parents took this news very badly, they felt Johny had misled and lied to them and were bitterly disappointed that he should have chosen a career in the army instead of what they had planned and been carefully working towards.

Initially there was a dearth of correspondence, with only the marquis writing to his parents admitting his guilt and asking for some measure of leniency. 'I shall endeavour to do everything else to your satisfaction that you may have as little reason as possible to grudge me being abroad.'[21] But this got no reply from his parents and the extent of their emotions at this time was shown in a letter from Katherine's brother the Earl of Orkney (who was one of the lieutenant generals in command under the Duke of Marlborough in Flanders), who wrote to Atholl with great concern, as he couldn't understand why he hadn't heard from either him or his sister on how they wanted him to advise his nephew:

> I was at the Hague when I saw my Ld Tullibardine and I can't but with concern write to you about him, its true I saw him at London and I am sure I never was more surprised in my life when he told me the manor he had left I doe assure you I dissuaded him all that lay in my power from following the projects he had in his head...

he relates how he had talked with him at length and also discussed his prospects with the Duke of Marlborough and, though he didn't think the situation was ideal, he was,

> ...of the opinion the Duke and Duchess should now give their consent as the alternative was very worrying and would do no good for the family but however now that he is come to the year of a man since his inclinations lead him to follow the war I wish you had given your consents I know this is talking like a mad man to my sister and I own I should not advise anybody to follow this way of life but yet I can't help thinking parents are to comply when they are told their bent and inclinations are that way.[22]

The marquis, unable to get the command he thought he would be given was, at this point, considering going to Italy, which Orkney was very concerned about as he had no idea how he intended to fund the trip and what extreme measures he may be tempted to take to get credit for it. With great difficulty he persuaded his nephew to stay where he was until he got a reply from the duke, and then asked both parents to give their son a chance as he had 'good spirit', and he was sure he would 'make a figure in the world'. Orkney played a crucial role at this point as family negotiator as, like his mother the Dowager Duchess, he clearly had great affection for the marquis but was also aware that his parents would be very upset by what he had done. His plea to his sister was very touching and again showed the strong family bonds, 'I hope she will act the mothers part and be tender and compassionate which

I dout not but will long run may be a better way to reclaime him than severity and may prevent more misfortune.'[23]

The duke's reply was uncharacteristically humble and honest as he admitted the reason he hadn't written was because he 'was ashamed to do it having gone away without my consent and that I could give no tolerable reason for such action.' Again, however, he pleaded with Orkney to try to persuade him not to take the path he had, 'the best advice your Lordship or any real friend can give him is to return to his father's house where he never wanted, nor shall want what is fit for his quality, if he return soon with a sense of fault in leaving me in such a manner for *la plus courte follie est la mellieure.*'[24]

Eventually the duke also wrote to his son explaining the lack of correspondence was due to him not taking his advice and that he had wanted him to learn that gaining the right post for his status wouldn't be as straightforward as he assumed it would be, 'it was not at all agreable to my inclinations that you should take yourself to that imployment which I am convinced is nether good for soul, body, or your circumstances in this world.'[25] His objections to his joining the army weren't limited to the fact that it wasn't suitable for one of his status, but it was also for fear of his physical and mental health and future prospects. However, despite another last-ditch plea that he spend his time studying instead, Johny ignored his father's advice and joined the Duke of Marlborough at Rouslar as one of his aide de campes, the first 'scotte man to have that favour'.[26]

From the camp at Heslein, between Tournay and Coutray, the marquis wrote to his father telling him that since joining Marlborough he had been 'civill eneugh', and distinguished him from the other aide de camps: 'I went with him to Ostend and was in the trnches the night before it surendered. Ther was very hot firing: the bombs from our battruis set fier to severall places of the toune at once.' He then went on to comment on the state of the land he was seeing. 'This is a every fine countrie, abounding in excellent fruits of all sorts and graine. All is spoilt where the armey comes, the trees broke in pulling the fruit, and cornes cut or trode downe which are just ripe. Evry camp spoils several thousand pounds worth besides what is usefull to men and horse.'[27]

The marquis' military life was not as straightforward as he had hoped; short of money, he was forced to make repeated requests to his parents for more. In October 1706 he wrote:

> I hear you refuse to pay the bill of two hundred pound I drew to enable me to apear at the armey like your son. This not only has been a great shame to me but puts me to extreem want ... I hope your Grace will consider these my very hard circumstances and not continue your anger for my coming away w'out your consent and my mothers which is what I will regrait more deeply all my life to have offended so kinde parents and dos aske pardon most humbly for it.[28]

The duke, who was in Edinburgh, informed Katherine at Dunkeld of this, but her reply to him was not very forgiving: 'I heartily pray God forgive him and bring him to a due sense of his sins which I confess I am not of the opinion he is yet arrived at.'[29] She was not at all happy he was requesting money and couldn't understand why he was claiming he hadn't got a post when they knew he had been given one. Significantly, she wasn't replying to her son herself, but only through her husband, even going so far as to write that the duke couldn't send him her blessing as she wasn't there! The confusion over Johny's appointment was explained later when he wrote to his father that because he had been given an appointment which usually went to the lieutenant colonel, half his pay was being taken from him to placate him.[30]

Johny wrote regularly to his parents during the campaign, though he didn't always receive a reply, although this was often due to the lack of a reliable delivery service. Also, his uncles Lord Orkney and Lord Edward Murray (a brother of the duke's who was also on the campaign), mentioned Johny in their letters, updating the duke on his progress and well-being. In September 1706 Lord Edward wrote:

> ... my nephew Tull is verie well he is always with the Duke of Marlborough or my lord Orkney they are putting in for a regiment for him my Lord Duke is much his friend in it I am hopeful he will get it, if he obtains it he may live verie handsomely ... and now the war by all appearance being near an end he will be in no

hazard of his person which I know will be comfortable to my dear brother and lady Duchess.[31]

Unfortunately, Lord Edward's view, of there being no hazard to his person, proved to be erroneous as tragically, despite Marlborough gaining a victory at the Battle of Malplaquet in 1709, Johny was killed. It was one of the bloodiest battles of not only this campaign, but the whole eighteenth century, with casualties from both sides numbering tens of thousands. This century had seen a dramatic development in the use of weapons and tactics from that of the previous ten to twenty years. All men in the infantry were now armed with flintlock muskets with socket bayonets. Battalions were divided into platoons firing in volleys which combined with the increased use and effectiveness of artillery meant the battlefield was dominated by gunpowder and bullets. When the Allies, consisting of a huge army of English, Dutch, Austrians, Hanoverians, Prussians and Danes, met the French and Bavarian forces on 11 September, the result was a bloodbath. Although initially hailed a hero, Marlborough was later criticised for his tactics on this day and the horrific loss of life.

At the battlefield Lieutenant John Fraser, formerly a servant of the Duke of Hamilton, wrote to Captain John Hamilton, announcing that the marquis had died that day, 'being first wounded in the thigh and then shot in the head.' He then listed other Scottish casualties but could write no more details, 'being just lookeing on my dear lord's corps',[32] except to add that the Earl of Orkney was safe. When Orkney, who had also been at the battle, wrote to the duke to give his account, he described how after Lord Tullibardine was 'shot throw the thigh he would not come off and showed more than ordinary courage.'[33]

When the news reached Scotland both the Murray and Hamilton families were utterly grief-stricken. One of the first family members to contact the Duke of Atholl was his brother-in-law the Duke of Hamilton:

I can't find words to alieviate your Grace's grief, or express my own for the irreparrable loss of your dear son Tullibardine the news of which is just now arrived here … next to yourself I am sure no body feels this with more sorrow than I doe whatever you may think assure yourself when you have occasion of any proofe of it you will find that to your person and family noebody has a more tender and faithful regard than my Lord your Grace's humble servant and afflicted brother Hamilton.[34]

From the countess of Dunmore, 'It's a thousand pities that so much bravery and other good qualities should be soe early cut off',[35] and Selkirk, 'I have not words to express my concerne for the irreparable loss your Grace and all of us have in dear Lord Tullibardine.'[36] Lord Edward from the camp at Haver wrote:

I am verie unfitt hand to give my dear brother the unwelcome and melancholie news of the death of my dear nephew, having so grate a shear of your loss that I am indeed skers able to express it. He was becom a verie fine gentellman and I may justly say wold have proved an honour to his countrie and family.[37]

In Hamilton, Johny's sister Susan, aged 10, wrote: 'my dear grandma is so very much afflicted for my brother that she has never been well since she had the account of his death.'[38]

The impact of his death at the time was significant both for the family and the people on the estates he was to have inherited, if not the country as a whole. We can safely assume that a young, tall, dashing heir, who had, in his youth, spent time in the Highlands of his home to learn their language and was particularly loved among his own family would have been a very popular and well liked figure. Written in 1714 by a schoolmaster in Glenshee, the following poem evokes a feeling of how significant a loss his death was felt by many in the area:

'Upon the never enough to be lamented death of the illustrious and noble John, Marquis of Tullibardine who departed this life at the Battle near Mons, the first of September 1709'

What sighs, what groans, are those I hear always?
What gushing torrents now run from all eyes?
What wofull news, what killing sound is this
That fills all hearts with grief and bitterness.

Blair Castle, Perthshire. (*Author's own image*)

Huntingtower, Perth, view looking north. (*Author's own image*)

Huntingtower, Perth. View looking south, only the two towers of the original castle now remain. (*Author's own image with permission of Historic Environment Scotland*)

John Murray, Duke of Atholl. (*Image from the collection at Blair Castle, Perthshire*)

Katherine Hamilton, Duchess of Atholl. (*Image from the collection at Blair Castle, Perthshire*)

Memorial in St Mary's, Kilmuir, Skye erected
to Lord Thomas Fraser, 10th Lord Lovat,
father of Simon, died at Dunvegan 1699.
(*Author's own image*)

Dowager Duchess Anne Hamilton. (*Alamy
Image*)

Lady Margaret Nairne. (*Alamy Image*)

John Murray, Marquis of Tullibardine died
at the Battle of Malplaquet. (*Image from the
collection at Blair Castle, Perthshire*)

William Murray, Marquis of Tullibardine. (*Image from the collection at Blair Castle, Perthshire*)

Lord George Murray. (*Image from the collection at Blair Castle, Perthshire*)

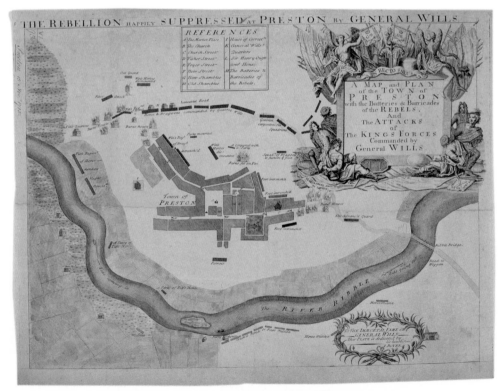

Battle of Preston. (*Royal Collection Trust/© Her Majesty Queen Elizabeth II 2019*)

Sheriffmuir. (*Author's own image*)

Gathering stone at Sheriffmuir where the Jacobites are said to have assembled before the battle. (*Author's own image*)

Map of the area around Sheriffmuir.
(*Alamy image*)

Picture of the Battle of Sheriffmuir here entitled the Battle of Dumblain (Dunblane) artist not assigned. (*Picture is on display at the Dunblane Museum and used with their kind permission*)

Scone Palace where James III briefly held court. Image shows the River Tay which froze over in 1716. (*Image Maddy Anderson 2019*)

Amelia Murray, wife of Lord George. (*Image from the collection at Blair Castle, Perthshire*)

Tullibardine Chapel where Lord George wanted to be interred with his wife and children. It stood next to Tullibardine Castle, of which there are no remains left. (*Author's own image*)

Sign at Sheriffmuir commemorating 300 year anniversary of the battle. (*Author's own image*)

Glenfinnan Monument, where William Marquis of Tullibardine, raised the standard marking the start of the 1745 Rising. (*Author's own image*)

> Ah Dolfull news! But they cannot be fled,
> The noble Marquis Tullibardin's dead.
> That sweet, that noble matchless paragon;
> Ah! is he gone? He's gone; alas he's gone.

Mr Robert Smith, Scottish Elegiac Verses 1629–1729

If this was how the locals and extended family felt, then it is no surprise that the duke himself was devastated. To experience so much grief in such a short space of time was almost too much for him to cope with. A month after the news had come through, Margaret Nairne took it upon herself to express the concern of both herself and that of his relatives:

> My lord and I are very sorry to find your grief still lyes so heavily upon you to the prejudice of your health your Grace has indeed within these last years met so great misfortune, the ruine of your country, the loss of an incomparable wife, a tedious imprisonment, a lingering sickness and at last the untimely death of an excellent son these are afflictions I think as great as humane nature can be trusted with … remember Lord what you owe to your excellent children, your family, your friends and your country who still hopes for great things from you, therefore do not disappoint so many expectations by indulging a sullen grief which alase cannot retrieve your loss but add to them that of your own for your Grace has a great heart yet you labour under a weakly body.[39]

She had asked for forgiveness in writing in such a manner, but felt the need to remind him of his duty.

Heartbroken and grieving, the duke had written to his second son William, who had now succeeded to the title of Marquis of Tullibardine, asking him to come home immediately, but had received no reply. Two months later the duke expressed his concern to Orkney writing: 'I am so full of anxiety for my son William from whom I have not heard these six months.'[40]

However William, who was at sea, was in no hurry to return and take on the burden of being the heir.

Chapter 8

William, Marquis of Tullibardine

William Murray was born 14 April 1689, three days after the crowning of King William and, no doubt, was named in his honour. He attended St Leonards' College at the University of St Andrews and in 1706 won the Silver Arrow, the much coveted archery prize.[1] He may have been successful in archery, but as his father notes later: 'you came from the school and college where I wish you have prospered more.'[2] The duke suggested he go abroad, to Utrecht for example, to learn French and improve himself and for this he also employed the services of a gentleman from Edinburgh, 'a gentleman that was recommended to me as a discreet and sober person to wait on you, not so much as a governor as a companion and to be assisting to you, which you would have found very useful in a foreign country.'[3] However, this gentleman suggested his time was being wasted and he should return to Edinburgh as William had other ambitions.

Not long after the death of his mother in 1707, the 18-year-old William expressed a desire to go to sea. The senior members of the family were not keen and strongly advised him against it. The Earl of Selkirk, at home in Hamilton with his mother Anne, wrote to the duke that he had witnessed everything said by the duchess, 'to dissuade your son Lord William from the thought of going to sea'.[4] He also had spoken to him but,

> … all to no purpose he has such a fixed desire and resolution to go to sea that there is no dissuading him from it so her Grace tho I am sure it is as much contrary to her inclination as yours sayes that if he were her son she would not be against his going fearing that if he be crossed in this which he is so bent upon the consequences may be fatal to him.[5]

However, he also suggested to the duke that William was more likely to succeed in this career if he had his father's recommendation than if he didn't.[6] In Anne's opinion, she had done all she could, but to no avail and now felt that she no longer wanted to discuss the topic, 'for it damps him and makes him melancholy'.[7]

The duke took the Hamilton's advice and reluctantly gave his consent, but not without sending William a lengthy letter of instructions on his conduct in which he, Atholl, asserted he had 'acted the part of a most loving and affectionate father.'[8] The letter began rather dramatically with:

My son William, since by your own choice you are now to leave me for a considerable time, perhaps never to meet here, because the common accidents and diseases and dangers which you may be exposed to or uncertain state of my health may deprive me of the comfort of ever seeing you again.

Therefore I think it is my duty to give you my instructions and advice in writing … frequently read them.

Included in these instructions are the efforts the duke considered he had taken to persuade him to stay, reasons why he shouldn't go to sea at all and advice on life and religion. The duke laid out the moral obligation of duty and his own life experiences, attempts by him to find a suitable wife for his son and claimed that as well as being a danger to his own person, a life at sea was unlikely to be profitable and more likely to mean he will be 'falling into evil company which is generally agreed are ordinarily more profligal at sea than at land which cannot be so easily shuned when you are tied to a ship as if you were on land, where you have more choice.'[9]

This was an emotional time for the duke. The union he was against had been passed into law, his relationship with his eldest son Johny was failing, his beloved wife had recently died and now his next son was refusing to do his duty and fulfil the role he had mapped out for him. The duke had hoped to have a better relationship with this son because he was so frustrated with the first who, 'without any ground or reason has chosen the part of the younger brother … he not only unnecessarily exposes himself abroad, but he has given me too great and too many causes of provocation and seems like Esau to despise his birthright.'[10]

William was determined, however, and he left for England in February 1708 to join the navy. In August he wrote to his father of how the fleet he was with had left Spithead, off Portsmouth, and sailed for France, taking part in an attempted invasion of the French coast. Ironically, this took place only a month after his father had been put under house arrest for supposed involvement in the 1708 Jacobite plot. By 1715 the allegiances of father and son were entirely different. In 1709 any career ambitions William may have had in the navy were dramatically cut short by the death of his elder brother as he, being next in line, inherited the title and responsibilities of being the heir to the Atholl estates.

The duke was very keen to have him in Scotland as soon as possible; he wrote to Orkney expressing his concern at not having heard from him: 'I am now full of anxiety for my son William, from whom I have not heard these six months, the last letter I had from him was from Port Mahon, I cannot but think there is some account about him by the last ships come from the streights.'[11] There was a genuine desire by the duke to have his son back home safe, not only to be with him, which he needed after the death of Johny, but he also wanted William to take up the role and duties associated with being heir, in a manner he could dictate.

However, it was obvious from the outset that William was reluctant. Obviously being at sea it would take some time for William to get the news and to then be physically able to return, but given his later actions it's also very likely he used this as an excuse to prolong his time away.

By August the following year there was still no news. The duke wrote again saying the death of his brother should, 'determine you to return home as soon as possibly you can for there is nothing more desirous than to see you returned soon and safe which I pray God grant that we have a comfortable meeting.'[12] The duke had read in the papers about the engagement with the French which had cause him 'a great deal of uneasings', but above all the letter stressed that whatever money was needed to bring William home he would pay, and that William should ask his captain for a loan, which the duke would settle, in order for him to return at the first opportunity; 'I long so much to have you with me which is fit for you especiallie since my loss of your eldest brother. Your affection and loving father.'[13]

William was to spend several months in Venice before he eventually did return to London in April 1711,[14] and a life he much preferred to what was waiting for him in Scotland. In London he could be away from the strict Presbyterian rule of his father, whose main intention now was for William to learn how to manage the estate and find a wife. During his life several suitable marriage proposals were initiated on his behalf; in 1712 Lady Betty Harley, daughter of Lord Oxford;[15] in 1714 to a daughter of the Duke of Ormond, and also in 1714 to Lady Mary O'Brian, a granddaughter to the Duchess of Beaufort,[16] but he never did marry.

Eventually William made the journey up to Scotland, staying with his grandmother at Hamilton, in August 1711, where he also met with his uncle, Lord Selkirk. His opinion of William was positive and he appeared to be quite supportive of him in an escalating dispute between father and son over money. 'I hope your Grace shall have great comfort in him for he is really a very fine gentleman and I hope he will in time be a support to you and your family.'[17]

In a letter from Duchess Anne to the duke, she announced Tullibardine's arrival and that he intended to stay for a fortnight, but she hoped he could be persuaded to stay longer as this would allow time for the duke to visit them and 'settle affairs betwixt you and him at my son Selkirks sight and myn', as he had promised he would. She also was 'glad to see him so hopefull a youth and doubt not but you and all concerned shall have much comfort in him.'[18] The duke never made it to Hamilton, but an agreement was made and Atholl was given particulars of it in a letter William then carried with him to Blair.

Despite this intervention by relatives, with the best of intentions, the stay did not go well. It seems there was a clash of characters; both had their own expectations of what the other ought to be doing and both were clearly stubborn as well non-communicative with each other. William wrote to Selkirk asking for his assistance, as in his opinion he had tried his best but was getting nowhere:

> I thought it fit to acquaint your Lordship that according to my Lady Duches (Hamilton) orders and your instructions I endeavoured as much as possible to humer my Lord Duke in things indifferent (and have streached in others) besides beeing allwise with him since he came from Hamilton, and in the main don my utmost to carry on as a son that did not complain, but, after all, these efforts are ineffectual and nothing is like to prouve of any advantage where there are such different interests, for the least thing that can bear a wrong construction is laid hold on.
>
> I shall be no longer abele to beare the maner I am treated and the afrunts that are daily put upon me.[19]

When reference was made later to this visit by Selkirk it was very negative,

> ... he found when he was last down many faire promises were made him and that when he was in Scotland his father was to give him a settlement but when he came there he found nothing was intended but in contrary was convinced it was not possible for him to live in the manner he behoved to do without being in greater variance with his father than when he lives here and at a greater distance from him.[20]

As a result of the duke's failure to keep to the agreement, it wasn't long after William returned to London that he started to run into debt. He clearly much preferred life in London, in fact he seems to have preferred life anywhere other than where his father was. The little time they spent together was dominated by disputes and complaints from the duke that William wasn't living up to his responsibilities, while William believed he could do not right in his father's eyes. In response to a suggestion that in London William was interfering against his father's interest, William replied it was 'a thing so contrary to nature that I presume to declare I never harboured in my breast such a thought for I esteem it my greatest honour as well as duty and interest to advance what I can anything that seems to be for your Graces service.'[21]

Away from his father in London, William's patron was no doubt his uncle, the 4th Duke of Hamilton who, resident at St James Palace, was one of the main political players in the court and society. After the death of Katherine, the Hamilton brothers had taken an active interest in their nephews' lives and perhaps this duke, who frequently caused anguish for his own parents, had a special fondness for a similar soul. This is speculation; they rarely wrote, but both were in London so perhaps didn't need to. But what is evident is that William was particularly upset when in November 1712, Hamilton was killed. He wrote to his father:

> I had yr Gr's letter dated from Edr and having nothing to trouble yr Gr with at present being in the greatest consternation at the death of the D. of Hamilton, who was killed this morning in a dewel with my Lord Mohune who likewise dayed upon the spote in hyde Park.[22]

The certainty that this uncle's death played a role in his later decisions was to be made clear by William's own declaration in 1715.

Even before Hamilton's death, however, William's relationship with his father had deteriorated significantly. The duke had made repeated pleas to William and other relatives to persuade him to come home to Scotland to take up his duties as heir and, no doubt, to stop running up debts in London, but they had fallen on deaf ears. William clearly didn't want to return and constantly made excuses for not being able to obey the command, based on the fact he didn't have enough money. He wasn't alone in this as by the end of 1714 his younger brother Charles was having similar difficulties.

Chapter 9

Charles and George

T he younger rebel brothers were Charles, born at Falkland on 24 September 1691, and George, born at Huntingtower on 4 October 1694. Both attended school at Perth Academy where their father had been sent in his youth, probably boarding at the school, even though the Murrays did have a town house property in Perth.[1] It was quite common for children of nobility to attend a school, and even with the family living nearby at Huntingtower, George, apparently only went home at the weekends.[2]

While at the school a notable incident occurred involving George and his cousin Lord Rollo. On Candlemass Day the pupils presented a gift to the master, the pupil who gave the most was declared king, and kingship carried with it certain privileges, including being carried by the other scholars through the streets in state and being able to pardon a criminal.[3] In a letter to his father 16 March 1710 Lord George says,

> I was in school this forenoon there was a grandson of Lady Rollos who was whipt and I, by the privaledge I received at Candlemas went to protect him but the school master would not allow me … he ordered me to sit down, that it was non of my business. After he had done me the afront I resined al the privaledges I had … I hope your Grace will not alow me to be so affronted and let me stay no longer at school.[4]

It's not known for certain what the outcome of this was but it's likely this was the time he sought sanctuary with the Nairnes. In the prologue to the *Jacobite General*, Katherine Tomasson wrote that he ran away from school in Perth to his uncle William's home. There are no incidents involving Charles, who out of all the brothers seems to be the one who took best to academia and was genuinely keen to continue his studies and improve his education.

In December 1711 George was sent to college in Glasgow with a tutor,[5] but by the end of May the following year the duke had taken him out, as it was reported, 'hes no grait inclination to be a scoler but rather inclyns to the armie.'[6] Charles remained in Perth, staying at Huntingtower where sadly he had the duty to report the death of his younger brother Basil, aged 7, to his father:

> As I wrote to your Grace last day of my dear brother Basil's being dangerously ill so I now have the sad account of his death to write and it having pleased the Almighty God to remove him out of this world about 3 this afternoon I wish this may be a warning to us all to prepare for death since we know not when and how soon it may come and if your Grace may be long preserved for a blessing to us which all alwise be the earnest prayer of, may it please your Grace your Grace's most obedient and most dutiful son Charles Murray.[7]

The duke had been particularly fond of Basil, the last child born to him and his late wife Katherine. Charles himself was also taken ill at this time but fortunately recovered.[8]

After spending some time in London both Charles and George left for Flanders in July 1712 to obtain commissions in the army.[9] Charles became a cornet, the lowest rank of commissioned officer in the cavalry to General Ross, a relative of Duchess Mary, while George was his ensign, the lowest officer rank in the infantry.[10] However it wasn't long before both were suffering the same issues their brother William, and previously Johny had – a serious lack of money. While in Ghent, only a month after arriving, Charles wrote:

> I have not a whole shirt on my bake for what with my bro George wearing of them since he came from Scotland & my own wearing now these two year there is hardly a thread of them together. I likewise want napkins to wash my face and hands which every body has but myself … it is verie uncomfortable to be in a strange countrie without money or credit.[11]

He goes on to explain his regimental clothes and saddle furniture were to be taken off his pay so that he wouldn't receive his full pay till they were accounted for and even pleaded that if the duchess, his stepmother, knew of his condition he was sure she would pity him. Of all her stepsons, Charles seems to have had the closest relationship with the new duchess and she had a genuine fondness for him. The other brothers, though always respectful, never expressed anything other than the courtesy which would have been expected.

In 1713 both Charles and George went to Dunkirk. Charles was fairly successful there, but keen to improve his French, asked to be able to go to Lille where he recognised he would have more success improving his competency in the language with French speakers rather than keeping the company of English speaking officers.[12] In May 1714 he went to Paris to attend the academy there.[13]

On several occasions the brothers were visited by their uncles who regularly informed Atholl of their nephews' progress. In January 1713 the Earl of Orkney who, though his lengthy military service had recently ended, was a time-served, battled-hardened, seasoned commander of troops. He wrote to the duke about George and wasn't very complimentary. In his opinion, 'he is extremely head strong and more capable of giving advice than taking it.'[14] Orkney had discovered George was in significant debt and thought he needed to spend more time on his writing and spelling. Orkney did concede that George had been ill, however, and that may account for the debts he had accrued, but his general opinion of him was not positive. Hearing of this report, George defended himself by explaining his need for extra expenses, i.e. having to buy a mourning suite (due to the Duke of Hamilton's death) and that he had been sick, but the general impression of both Orkney and Selkirk was that George needed to be placed under tighter supervision and should have someone with authority to look over him.

George seems to have suffered ill health on a number of occasions throughout these years and eventually the duke wrote to Anne from London that he intended to, 'send for George from Dunkirk which is a very unwholesome place, that he may come here and stay as long as I doe and larne his exercises in this place for I heare he learns nothing there.'[15] In 1713 George returned to England, staying in London where he became quite settled, though he suffered an illness again in 1714. He visited his grandmother in June at Hamilton where she dispensed what was to become her routine advice and instructions to her grandson. She wrote to his father about the visit saying he was 'so hopeful a youth', and that, 'I am very hopeful that what you have lay'd out or shall further give him you shall think well bestowed and have comfort and satisfaction in.'[16] She naturally had a soft spot for George as, 'everybody hear think Lord George lyk his mother, God make him a good man, as she was a woman.'[17] At Hamilton Palace it would be difficult to give anyone higher praise than to liken him to such a beloved member of the family.

In 1714 Anne had suggested to Atholl that Orkney should be asked to help George advance his career, but Atholl wasn't keen; he had other plans at this stage for George. Anne couldn't understand why the offer was turned down as she was sure Orkney would have done all he could to help. It was perhaps that Atholl's intention was to keep George out of military life and Orkney's involvement would have been contrary to that aim. Instead, George was employed to act on behalf of his father in London while the duke was in Scotland and, as part of that role, Geroge arranged for miners from Germany to be brought over to work for the duke at his holdings in Blairingone and Solsgirth in what is now Clackmannanshire. In 1715 he wrote: 'your Grace was very well satisfied with my management of the miners which I am glad of since I did what was thought best for your Grace's service.'[18] This interest and involvement in the family mines continued in later years when he wrote lengthy letters to his brother James, the 2nd Duke, on the subject. Following this success George wrote thanking his father for agreeing to pay a bill he had sent to him and added: 'I believe I have not yet acquainted your Grace that his Majesty some months ago ordered I should be appointed paymaster to the lottery.'[19] While George clearly seemed to have found a niche he was successful at and was benefiting from an improved relationship with his father, the situation was very different for that of his brothers William and Charles.

From 1713 onwards the letters between Anne, her sons Lords Selkirk and Orkney, and grandsons William and Charles became increasingly dominated by their lack of money and Atholl's seeming intransigence in either providing the brothers with a basic allowance or paying off any debts they had accrued. Orkney and Selkirk were under the impression the duke could afford to give his sons more, as Atholl had received payment of the arrears from the government he had been chasing for a number of years. They thought Charles at least managed on a pittance and though none of their nephews were blameless, their opinion was that the duke's austere attitude was instrumental in causing increasing family strife and bitterness.

At first their correspondence was mostly concerned with William who, staying in London, refused to go back to Scotland despite repeated commands by his father. The tone of disapproval from the duke gradually increased, but William was determined not to return until a promise of settling his debts was agreed. Atholl, realising he was getting nowhere with his stubborn son, wrote to his mother-in-law and asked her to intervene:

> My son Tullibardine never writes anything of his leaving London notwithstanding my repeated advice & command to do it he still complains of wanting mony ... I entreat your Grace might be pleased to write to him to come home and whatever he desires that is reasonable shall be done.[20]

The Earl of Selkirk wrote to his mother January 1714:

> I must say that it is a great misfortune the son is not a little more complaying with his father and that may to endevour to gaine him ... if there could be an end put to the uncertaine and unhappy condition of this young man one might hope he would think of turning himself to something and as he is it incapasitates him from doing anything.[21]

Lord Selkirk had previously written to the duke with his advice and proposed,

> 500 a year to your son Tullibardine ... and I hope may do more towards the reclaiming of him than harsh measures for your

Grace knows his humour and how high a spirited youth he is. I am sure it is not to be expressed the condition I left him in when I came last from London and how uneasy it was for me to see one of his quality and necessity he was in without money or credit.[22]

Atholl later acknowledged Lord Selkirk had done his best to help, 'I cannot but own my Lord Selkirk has done the part of a kind relative in persuading him which I hope will at last take effect.'[23]

But by the end of the year Selkirk was clearly losing patience with William himself. He felt he had done his best to persuade him to go back to Scotland, including the suggestion that the duke, his father, send £50 for travel expenses and give him another £50 when he get there. However, this plan came with the caveat that the money be sent to Selkirk, to act as a 'purse master' who would control the spending of it. This didn't gone down well with William, but Selkirk had refused to write on any other terms.[24]

Despite his efforts at negotiation, Selkirk came to the conclusion only his mother Anne would be able to resolve the tension building between the two. 'I find his only hope is from your Grace's assistance and that by your interest with his father you will prevail with him to make some reasonable settlement on his son.'[25] Clearly this was a role at which the whole family felt Anne excelled. As Katherine had done years before with Johny, so now Atholl also thought his mother-in-law would be the key player in resolving their issues:

I am in hopes my son Tullibardine may come down before that time who gave me his word before my Lord Selkirk that he would come down with him. When he is before your Grace I hope he will be advised to enter into measures to make me and himself easier in time coming than we have been hither to with his too long staying at London.[26]

However, by this stage it wasn't just William the uncles were concerned about as their letters increasingly included Charles, whose situation had become even more desperate. Lord Selkirk recently back from France wrote to Anne:

I see a letter writ by your Grace order to my brother Orkney in relation to my Lord Tullibardine I have been speaking to him on the same subject he tells me he is willing to come to Scotland providing his father send him where with all to clear his debts here and make his journey. I wish with all my heart he were from this and that there were some settlement made betwixt his father and him and he tells at present he has not one farthing of money nor does he know where to gett any he has been asking me but I told him I had no money to lend him and I am on this subject I cannot but informe your Grace of the condition I left Lord Charles Murray at Paris being wholly destitute of money either to pay his dinner or pay his masters ... it is rally a pity he should not finish his exercise for he was doing very well and very moderat in his expenses.[27]

Not long after his arrival in Paris, Charles had requested more money from his father, 'contrary to his inclinations', he had had to draw a bill on the Duke of Atholl for £80. 'I confess your Grace gave me enough before I left London, but I had the misfortune to spend the best part of it there which I ought not to have done and for which I hope your Grace will forgive me.'[28] This was the start of a saga which was to sow the seed for future disharmony between father and son as Charles' need for money increased; receiving no reply from Atholl he continued to make false assumptions and accusations. Initially he accepted he wasn't innocent of blame, he shouldn't have spent the money in the way he did and, as recompense, he detailed how he would pay his father back, including giving him the payment of arrears he was due as an officer. However, despite this apology and suggestion to remedy it, further requests for aid received no reply. Charles' letters then rapidly escalated in urgency and emotion as he became more desperate for an answer. He needed the money to pay for his next term at the college and was embarrassed by the constraints in which he found himself; 6 August 1714:

I finde to my unexpressable grief I can propose myself to stay here noe longer I certainly would never have left London if I had in the least thought it would run so hard with me as I find it has done but I came here full of hopes if your Grace wou'd have answer'd my first and only bill that I ever drew upon you without your consent.[29]

Three days later, still with no reply, he wrote:

I wish to God your Grace had never given me a farthing to have come abroad on rather than after I came to be reduc'd to such hardships and extremity (& all this to happen for poor 80 pound) so that I have become the talke of Paris, which is a reflection too severe, neither is my concern for myself only I am sorry likewise that your Grace's reputation shou'd suffer through me, which last vexes me more than anything I could have happened to.[30]

A few days later Charles wrote again, his sixth letter without a reply; he had asked Selkirk for money but had been refused and had been offered money by an (unnamed) Irishman who had then also turned him down. He had been granted time by the master of the academy, who didn't want to set a bad example of a pupil leaving in debt, and fortunately his cousin Basil's governor had spoken for him. However, he was quite distraught and wrote: 'I hope I never did anything that could have deserved such a very hard wage I had rather die than undergoe it again.'[31]

On 20 August a reply was sent by the duke with the simple statement that he had written at the beginning of the last month saying he had accepted that first bill. In his letter he showed little tolerance for the drama and emotional tone of Charles' letters, but then he had a very different understanding of the situation.

I am sorry to hear of the hardship you have layen under, but I hope it will have done good effect, as to make you follow my advice in time coming for you can not but know how much it was against my inclination your going to France and that I offered to pay your charges in ryding in Mr Huberts acacdemy at London but your answer was that if I would give you a hundred pound you would ask no more for a year and which sume you know you received and more before you went. All I shall now say is that the sooner you return from it the better I believe you have learn'd as much French as to understand, *La plus courte follie est la mellieure.*[32]

It was during this time that Charles had received a visit from Lord Selkirk who was in Paris on behalf of his mother, Anne. When Selkirk returned to London he confirmed that he had met up with Charles and, though he had no money to lend him, had agreed to contact his father on his behalf as he was,

> … wholly destitute of money either to pay his dinner or pay his masters he was traying to get as much as needs him over but I desired he lay those thoughts asaid since it was a pity to loss the beginning and progress he had made in his exercise.[33]

By this time, however, due to the dramatic change of affairs in the country, Atholl now wanted all his sons home.

Chapter 10

The Death of Queen Anne

By August 1714, two events had irrevocably changed the dynamics of the Murray family, forcing commitment and acting as a catalyst to the deteriorating relationship of the duke with his sons. The first was that in 1712 the duke had been appointed Lord High Commissioner to the General Assembly, the sovereign's personal representative to the Annual General Assembly of the Church of Scotland. In this post he attended the General Assembly of the Church of Scotland on behalf of the sovereign, made the opening and closing addresses to the Assembly and carried out a number of official functions. It was a role he took very seriously as he saw it as his duty to uphold the state religion. It was inevitable, then, that his attitude to known Episcopalians who weren't praying for their sovereign would now be less tolerant – and more so in the near future, as being Episcopalian was seen as a direct indicator of being Jacobite. The first sign of his more strict attitude was shown in 1713 when he wrote that his own brothers, 'James and Lord Nairne have set up a meeting house where the minister does not pray for the Queen, but for their sovereign ... I have writ both to the Treasurer and Earl of Mar to acquaint the Queen of it to know what course shall be taken.'[1] This was significant as he clearly knew he had to act now, even with relatives, rather than sit on the fence. However, it was the death of Queen Anne that triggered the cycle of events which led to the total collapse of family harmony.

The duke had been kept informed of the queen's illness by several people in London, including his sons William and James and the Earl of Mar, who wrote frequently keeping him up to date as her condition deteriorated.

The council earnestly recommends to your Grace to do what you can for preserving the peace and quiet of the country and particularly where your grace has most interest which I make no doubt will be your care, God preserve our peace and quiet and grant your Grace his direction.[2]

Later the same day Mar wrote again: 'I hope in God our countrymen will be wise and not run our country into a field of blood and confusion.'[3]

Queen Anne died on 1 August 1714. James, the duke's loyal son, wrote that he had been in charge of the guard and had to stay close when she died, 'tho it is true so good and gracious a sovereign can never be enough regretted, I am very sensible that for my particular I have lost the best of Mistresses.'[4] The government ministers moved rapidly to ensure the Hanoverian succession went through without any issues. Concerns for a rising in favour of James III were very real and the Lords Justice acted quickly to prepare for this. The Habeas Corpus Act was suspended, so suspects could be detained without trial and the Riot Act was passed, which allowed for any group of twelve or more people unlawfully assembled to be dispersed. The Security of the Sovereign Act was also passed, which ordered all office holders, either civil or military, peer or commoner, to appear before His Majesty's court and publicly swear an oath of allegiance to him and to the church.

Anne's successor, George I, son of Sophia of Hanover, was unpopular with many from the start. Unable to speak any English, he arrived in London with his two mistresses and proceeded to appoint a very Whig cabinet which excluded and annoyed many leading Tory nobles.

For a while the James VIII's supporters assumed they would have an ally in the Duke of Atholl and getting him to commit to their cause was initially their main aim:

These lords have suspicion of Atholl on good grounds, but yet they are humbly of opinion that your Majesty should take no step in this particular which may give him pretence for deserting your service, and therefore, that a mark of confidence may be shown him which will be extremely soothing to a man of his natural temper ... they propose that two commissions may be returned signed by your majesty, one appointing Atholl to command, but obliging him to act by the advice of Mar, Marishall and two or three more of your friends there such as you think deserve that trust and the other entirely blank. In case Atholl will accept of the commission and enter heartily into your service, the second commission will never be produced.[5]

This offer of the post of General to Atholl had first been suggested by Earl of Mar in July 1715.

But whether this was actually offered or not, it never happened. Instead, Atholl's official view was that, 'The Queen's sudden death is a great loss to these nations; I am particularly concerned in it having been particularly obliged to her. It is a mercy that we have a Protestant King to succeed her.'[6]

The duke was urged by several friends and acquaintances to make the journey to London or Edinburgh to show his support for the new king. John Douglas in Edinburgh wrote, 'so for God sake my Lord it's expected impatiently your Grace coming here at all expedition, for most of our quality of all ranks are coming in and your having the honour to be first minister of state in this place, all their eyes are upon you.'[7] And Lieutenant General Ross: 'I hope you pardon me if I venture so far as to say that I think you should come immediately to this place that you may waite on the King at his arrival and offer his majesty your service which I do not doubt will be acceptable.'[8] But Atholl saw his role as being in Perthshire to keep the peace. This action could, of course, be interpreted as hedging his bets to wait out future events, but as he must have been aware of a potential rising, he also knew, from past experience, that he needed to be in the best position to defend his estate: 'I will be obliged to stay now for a longer time in this country that I may keep the peace in it for your Grace knows what troubles happened after King William's succession to the crown, my father being out of the country and I residing at Falkland.'[9]

In the same vein, the opinion of the elder Hamilton and Murray family members was that the Murray brothers should go to their posts as soon as was practical, to show their loyalty to the new king. The duke informed his son Charles 'I believe you may have seen by the prints that the Justices have ordered all officers in Ireland immediately to report to there respective commands.'[10]

Charles returned to London from France in December 1714 but was clearly resentful that the progress he felt he had been making had been cut short due, in his opinion, to lack of funds:

> I came here from France last night, where I went with a design to have improven myself in which I have not succeeded as I expected and design I cannot say I was anyways capable of improvement but tho I had I must needs say my very narrow allowance would have obstructed it.[11]

He had apparently asked for an allowance of £25 expecting, by being so modest in his request, to be given more – double in fact. However, the duke was now clearly of the opinion he needed no more as he was due to rejoin his regiment in Ireland and in the meantime should come back to Scotland. It was in this atmosphere, with a clear undercurrent of discontent, that Charles returned to the family home at Blair Castle in February 1715.

Perhaps unsurprisingly then, it wasn't long before the relationship was tested and a heated discussion was had over the provision of his allowance. In July Charles stormed out of Blair; this was followed by a very impassioned exchange of letters, which clearly upset both father and son:

> When I came from London it was with a resolution to have stayed with your Grace till I should be in a condition to go to the regiment in Ireland and I thought when all things failed me I could have bread at home but I find it is the first thing that has failed me, what may be the reason or who is the cause that I am forc'd from thence I shall not say but to my comfort this I can say I have done nothing to deserve it I shall be your grace's obedient and dutifull son.[12]

Apparently, the duke received an apology for this letter, but he was clearly quite shocked by it. Charles was welcomed at Hamilton where they had some sympathy for his plight, having had so many positive reports on him from Orkney and Selkirk. At Hamilton they put Charles' outburst down to his youth. Anne Montgomery, the Dowager Duchess' housekeeper, wrote to Atholl in Charles' defence saying: 'I think him the sweetest tempered youth ever I saw and many things about him being engaging I often think he has a great deal of the kind temper of the late Lord Tulybardin whom I own I was very fond of.'[13] This, however, wasn't the sentiment of his father and after Charles' departure the duke sent his explanation of events to Anne:

> … your Grace will see by the enclosed letter he sent me the very day he parted last from me how extremely undutifull and egregiously unjust he is to me … all I said was that I agreed in your Grace's opinion as reasonable for him, otherways I shuld have been very well pleased he had stayed longer. I am blamed by all my friends for keeping my sons too much at home and being indulgent to them, there is some truth in this but to be at the same time blamed for forcing any of them away and not giving them bread is hard to heare from any especially from one of them. I have met with injustice and reproaches from many but never so much from any as my son Charles as you will see by another letter of his … few fathers would have been so indulgent as to have sent him mony to come home after such a letter … His brother Tullibardine bills have been protested against me and are not yet paid and as for Charles coming here again in the temper he is in it can be little satisfaction to him as well as me.[14]

Perhaps more worrying for the duke, however, was the fact the disagreement was not just about money but also religion, and this dispute wasn't just with Charles either:

> I hope what your Grace has said to Charles about his not receiving the sacrament lately with me will have good affects in time coming and that he will not neglect it when he has such another opportunity but I suspect that both he and his eldest

brother have taken up a prejudice to the Presbyterian way and that they have engaged to one another not to comply in receiving that way, perhaps he may be brought to acknowledge this to your Grace ... I told him that those remitted so plaine and expressely commanded duty to God would neither prosper in this world nor expect Gods favour in the next without a speedy and sincere repentance and amendment. Nor could it be expected that one that neglected duty to God but would also do it to their parent.[15]

The duke ended this letter with, 'I have writ to the Earl of Orkney concerning my son George if your Grace pleases to do it also it will have more effect.' By this stage he knew he couldn't keep George from taking a military post. Neither knew then, however, that the next letter the duke would receive from Charles would be his most dramatic and serious; a plea to save him from execution.

In August 1715, just a month after Charles' departure and following repeated commands from his father, William eventually arrived at Blair, the rumour being that the Earl of Mar has paid off his debts. Mar had been snubbed in the new round of appointments by King George. Nicknamed 'Bobbin John' for his tendency to change allegiance, Mar had instead chosen to pin his colours to the mast of James III and lead a Jacobite Rising. For this he needed to secure support from all leading nobles and if Atholl wasn't prepared to lead his men in support of a Stuart king, then his son would.

William's return was reported in a memorial, unsigned:

Saturday last the 13th instant the Marquis of Tullibardine arrived at Blair of Atholl to the great surprise of the Duke his father, he came post from London did not stope at Edinburgh tis certain he had no money from his father since our last yet he has plenty both of gold and money which appeared by his giving it to the country people very liberally.[16]

According to this writer the Lords Nairne and Strathallan were with Tullibardine and all refused to go to church or pray for King George, despite Atholl's efforts to persuade them to do so. Clearly the arrival of Tullibardine in the area was seen as significant because, whether Mar had paid his debts or not, his rebellious views were known to many if not his father.

When William arrived at Blair the duke was, at first, surprised but delighted. The visit started well as the duke,

> ... received him with all the marks of affection and kindness that any father can have for a son. I had forgot his former undutifullness & not obeying my repeated commands in coming home sooner. I confess my heart warmed to him and I must say his I think did to me; but alas this great happiness was not long lasting for about half an hour later...

Everything changed. William told him he was there by the king's command (meaning King James), 'I was perfectly struck with surprise at such an answer.'[17] The duke then recounted the gradual breakdown of the visit, including William walking three miles on foot to attend an Episcopal service, despite being banished to his room!

This was crisis point as far as Atholl was concerned, he was well aware how his son's actions would be perceived by others, especially as in the round of new appointments in 1714 he himself had lost his post as Lord Privy Seal. However, the following year he was made Lord Lieutenant of Perthshire, with the job of keeping the peace in the area for the government and stamping out any rebellious activity. At the time of his appointment he was assured by Lord Townshend, the future Secretary of State for the North, that, 'the King is extreamly satisfied & pleased with your assurance you have given him of your loyalty and affection to his person and government ... your Grace may depend upon his taking all occasions of giving your Grace further marks of his favour.'[18] He had made his decision on where his loyalties lay and didn't want his son's actions to jeopardise this.

In what had now become his usual method of dealing with his recalcitrant sons, the duke sent William, accompanied by George, to Duchess Anne. He hoped she could talk sense into him, as he assumed she had done with Charles and that she would ensure that both Charles and George went to their respective posts in the army, in Ireland. 'His Majesty orer'd all the officers then in the Army (and all Governors of Forts and garrisons, and other Officers of his army in Ireland) to repair immediately to their respective posts, upon pain of his highest displeasure.'[19] But that didn't happen. Instead, on 22 August 1715 after leaving Blair, William and George headed first to Faskally, where they contacted their cousin the Master of Nairne: 'this is to tell you that the good Elector of Ranoch*, Lord George and I are come here this night on our way to Mar and have sent this express to know what accounts you have of things'[20] and then North, to Braemar and the start of the Great Rising.

---

* (Struan Roberston)

Chapter 11

The Rising Begins

Despite the precautions taken for a smooth transition to the new Hanoverian monarchy, there had been growing unrest in several areas of England which continued after George's coronation. On 23 April 1715, pretending to observe the anniversary of Queen Anne's coronation, a crowd of people 'took occasion to make a tumult in London where they displayed a flag, beat their drum broke down windows wounded some loyal and religious persons with flint stones of considerable weight.'[1] This was followed a month later, on the birthday of King George, by a mob in Oxford composed of, 'gown-men belonging to the University... in a riotous and tumultuous manner, they raged from one part of the City to another breaking windows, rising houses and committing great outrages, to the terror of the inhabitants.'[2] June also saw disturbances as mobs assembled to toast the birthday of 'the Pretender' James. Incidents were reported in Somerset, Wolverton, Marlborough, Warrington and Leeds. A larger mob assembled in Manchester where 'they committed many ravages on the houses of those who were well affected to his Majesty's person and government.'[3] These riots and protests weren't necessarily pro-Jacobite and certainly didn't prove any commitment to the cause, but did give the impression of strong anti-Hanoverian sentiment, which encouraged James and his supporters to believe there was an opportunity that should now be taken.

James had made his views known at Anne's death, declaring that the current social situation was a republic and not a proper monarchy as appointed by God:

In such an extraordinary and importance conjucture in which not onely our Hereditary Right to our crowns is so unjustly violated ... everybody knows that the revolution of the year 1688 ruin'd the English monarchy and lay'd the foundation of a Republican government by devolving the sovereign power on the people who assembled themselves without any Authority, voted themselves a parliament and assumed themselves without authority and assumed a Right of deposeing and electing Kings ... from all which it is plain our people can never enjoy any lasting peace or happiness till they settle the succession again in the right line and recall is the immediate lawfull heir.[4]

This view carried some weight. George was not popular, but monarchy was still the preferred social order; the alternative having been rejected after the experience of the Commonwealth under Cromwell. By 1715 there had been five changes of monarchy in the previous thirty years, it wasn't unreasonable, therefore, to think another was feasible. James also had the backing of Louis XIV who naturally supported the divine right of kings, but had also personally committed to helping James on his father's deathbed.

In Scotland there was the additional factor of opposition to the established church, a main aim of many Jacobites being the restoration of the Episcopal church. Even today, particularly in Scotland, the Jacobite rebellions are thought of as being Roman Catholic against Protestant when in fact the majority of the rebels were Episcopalian. The Roman Catholic image was intentionally re-enforced in London by anti-papal pageants, including 'pope-burning' ceremonies, which had been revived by the Whigs at the end of Queen Anne's reign and continued during and after the rebellion. These were engineered for the specific purpose of associating Catholicism with James and the Tory rebels. Presbyterians too, especially the ministers, would always refer to the Jacobites as papists.[5]

James himself was a Catholic, but aware this may discourage Protestants from joining their cause, the Jacobite leaders frequently went out of their way to ensure non-Catholics were given prominent roles in both 1715 and 1745 risings. The Murray brothers were classic examples of the fact that Jacobite support in Scotland was mostly Protestant, none showed any inclination to become Catholic but at least two had begun to attend Episcopal church services rather than the Presbyterian services with which they had been brought up. There were Catholic supporters of the Jacobites, particularly from the Highlands, and clearly one of their motives would have been the benefits a Catholic monarch would bring. However, the main focus of discontent in Scotland in 1715 was opposition to the Union of 1707.

Having been promised economic benefits and assured of advantages by agreeing to the Treaty, nothing had so far materialised to show the majority of the population that union had been the right decision. In fact, taxes had increased on salt and linen, and in 1713 the proposed introduction of a malt tax led to riots, as it was perceived to be a direct infringement of the Treaty. The extent of feeling against the Union was demonstrated in 1713, when a motion made in the House of Lords to repeal it was supported by the Duke of Argyll and the Earl of Mar, both of whom had previously been strong advocates of it. Mar later wrote that, 'When I found that we (in Scotland) continued to be ill treated under the Union, I became as much for having it broke as ever I had been in earnest for having made it.'[6] A lively debate followed, but was ultimately rejected, although only by a very small majority. All that was needed then to harness this growing anti-Hanoverian and anti-union sentiment was effective leadership and a bit of luck, unfortunately for the Jacobites, in 1715 both were severely lacking.

John Erskine, the Earl of Mar had inherited estates in 1689 that were heavily in debt and reduced in size, but he had retained the sense of entitlement to a high status in society due to his ancestors' hereditary role of keepers of Stirling Castle and guardians of the royal princes. Initially a strong supporter of the Union, a view he moderated later, he was chosen as one of the Scottish representative peers, and in 1713 appointed Secretary of State for Scotland. At the time of Queen Anne's death, his allegiance had been with the Tory party, so he knew he would need to work to gain a position with the new king as well as trying to recover the £6,000 salary he was owed. However, he famously received a royal snub; George apparently turned his back on him at court and, with little prospect of a political future as well as mounting debts, he threw in his lot in with the Jacobites. In August 1715, fearing arrest after the discovery of plans for a rising in the south of England, he took ship and headed to Scotland.

Mar has received considerable criticism for his role in the 1715 Rising and there can be no denying he wasn't the right man for the role he took on, but the Jacobites weren't spoilt for choice. Writing of events later in his memoir, John Sinclair's view against him was very extreme, but then he had little positive to say about anyone: 'His original sin, both by his father and mother giving him as small a title to honour as estate, he soon gave himself up, as by instinct, to his hereditarie and naturell penchant, villanie and lying.'[7] Mar doesn't emerge well from any narrative on the 1715 rebellion, but he wasn't a military commander. Instead Mar was a consummate court politician who had also, for some years, managed to develop a reputation as a skilful amateur architect and garden designer. Many among the Scottish nobility deferred to his knowledge for advice on their estates. He also contributed to projects of the English aristocracy, including Bretton Hall and Rokeby Park in Yorkshire.[8] Not the usual qualifications for a military strategist. But what was to make his appointment in Scotland worse was his disastrous choice of military commander in England, Thomas Forster MP.

Mar had arrived at his estate in Braemar on 20 August 1715 after leaving London the week before, quickly making his way north via Newcastle, Edinburgh and Fife. There under the guise of a tinchal, a gathering for a hunt, he met with leading nobles and clan chiefs to organise the rebellion. The nobles then left to gather their men and reassemble some days later on 9 September, in the small market town of Kirkmichael, where James III was proclaimed king and his standard raised in Bannerfield. They moved from there to Moulin, then Logierait and then Dunkeld, moving south through the lands of Atholl. By this stage they already had a sizeable force and as their supporters had at this time taken Perth, they made the decision to make it their headquarters. A strategically important town commanding passage over the Tay, it also lay within easy access of coastal Fife and its many ports from which the rebels expected to be able to get supplies, particularly of weapons.

On the move to Perth, Mar was joined by William and George Murray leading a force of Atholl men. From Kirkmichael Mar wrote:

... the D. of Athole we hear has drawen his men together wh. will save us some trouble – he intended to stope my march, but his men have sent word that they will all join us to-morrow and leave his Grace. Lord Tullibardine and his brother Lord George are come to us already and some other of the gentlemen and, just as I am writing, we have an express sent us that 300 of the D of Athole's men hearing of Ld Tullibardine's coming here have left him immediately and they have sent to Lord T. since he came here to tell him they wait his commands where to join us and before to morrow night we are sure off the men he has.[9]

Many Atholl tenants supported the marquis, and the duke was unable to do anything other than make a stand at Blair Castle to ensure it too wasn't taken by the rebels. Having turned down a request to join them, it was clear to the duke that he needed to show unwavering commitment to the government to compensate for the rebellious actions of his sons. In a letter to Anne he wrote 'these actions of theirs will bring me under suspicion to the government as if I connived them which I am sure those that know me will believe I am not capable of.'[10] He actively sent out many letters by express to John Campbell, 2nd Duke of Argyll who had been sent to command the government troops in Stirling, and to minsters in London, to keep them appraised of the situation in Perthshire, making suggestions of what should be done to stop the rebels' progress. It was noted in London that the duke was making every effort to show his loyalty. The Earl of Nottingham, Lord President of the Council, wrote:

The King received very graciously the repeated assurances which your grace gave me in yours of the fifth instant of your fidelity to his Majesty and your zeal in his service; and is so far from imputeing to your Grace the criminal indiscretion of your son that he would gladly shew his mercy towards him, if he would yet render himself a proper object of it by his returning from those who are no less emenys of their countrey then of his Majesty.[11]

The Duke of Atholl, as Lieutenant of Perthshire, committed to raising six regiments of Highlanders for King George and sent four companies of his men to Perth to assist the provost there, but the provost felt the men's loyalty couldn't be trusted so they were sent back. Argyll himself was never wholly convinced of Atholl's reliability, never mind that of the Atholl men, often making accusations that the duke could not be trusted. Argyll wasn't in a position of strength at this stage, however; he was aware the rebel forces were increasing, but he didn't have nearly enough men to engage them. Since his arrival in Stirling, he had quickly come to the conclusion that ministers in London were seriously underestimating the situation in Scotland. There quickly developed a north-south divide between the government in London and its representatives in Scotland over both the urgency for action and the strength of the rapidly increasing rebel army. In London, a possible threat in the south was considered far more real, at least initially, than what may be happening in Scotland.

In stark comparison to Mar, Argyll was regarded as a man of his word and was a known, experienced, military commander, having taken part in the Wars of the Spanish Succession under Marlborough in 1702 and again in 1708–10 when he fought with Johny, the then Marquis of Tullibardine, at Malplaquet. As the Campbell chief he was not only head of one of the most powerful clans, but also the strongest supporter of the Hanoverian government in Scotland. John Mackay, a contemporary, was very complimentary: 'Few of his years hath a better understanding, nor a more manly behaviour. He hath seen most of the courts of Europe is very handsome in person fair complexioned.'[12] While Lockhart of Carnwarth's opinion was:

> His head ran more upon the Camp, than the Court; and it would appear nature had dressed him up accordingly, being altogether incapable of servile dependency and flattering insinuations requisite in the last and endowed with that cheerful lively temper and personal valour esteemed and necessary in the other.[13]

In Flanders, Argyll's relationship with Marlborough had soured and, after a brief return to London, he was sent to Spain as commander-in-chief of the British forces there, but his campaign wasn't particularly successful and he returned to court in 1713. In contrast to Mar, however, the accession of King George improved his fortunes as he was called on to take command in Scotland and put down the rebels.

During the next weeks of September, rebel forces in their thousands centred on Perth, including 1,400 Atholl men who were to be formed into four regiments commanded by the Marquis of Tullibardine, Lords Charles and George Murray and Lord Nairne.[14] Aware Tullibardine and Charles were both involved, it took longer for the penny to drop with the duke that George had joined too. On 2 September he was still under the impression George had, after an initial show of disobedience, done as he was ordered to and gone to Ireland: 'last account I had of my son Tullibardine was, that he was with the Earle of Mar and that George after being a night there went towards Irland to his post.'[15] Less than a week later it appears reality had dawned as he wrote: 'where George has gone I could not heare till 2 days since I had account he came back to Dunkeld and gave out he was going to Blair but I have not seen him nor is it fit I should after such unaccountable proceedings.'[16]

As the numbers in Perth steadily increased, Argyll's letters and pleas for assistance from England also became more urgent. To Lord Stanhope (Secretary of State for the southern department) he wrote:

> I am exteamly surprised that notwithstanding the advices you have had from hence, we have heard nothing either from Lord Townshend or you. And pardon me to say I am yet more surprised to find by a letter I yesterday received from London that his Majesty's Minister still persist to think this matter a jest and that we are in a condition to put a stop it it. Give me leave to say, Sir, that if all of us who have the honour to serve his majesty here are not either knaves or cowards, we ought to be believed when we tell you that his country is in the extreemest danger.[17]

Three days later he wrote again asking to be replaced as commander of the army since he felt that only then would reinforcements be sent; he was 'insisting on considerable reinforcements for without it or a miracle not only this country will be utterly destroyed but the rest of his Majesty's dominions put in the extremest danger.'[18] Clearly utterly disaffected, in this same letter he also took the opportunity to cast doubt on Atholl's loyalty, describing how money sent to Atholl had been intercepted by Tullibardine and though he found this suspicious, he had sent another £100, 'Lest he should take the pretence of want to deliver up his castle.'[19]

In Edinburgh, Lord Justice Clerk Adam Cockburn (the second most senior judge in Scotland), had been concerned for some time that the country was unprepared. Writing to the Duke of Montrose he felt they were an abandoned people, they needed troops and, although some shires had men, they didn't have ammunition. Back in August 1715, he had heard a report of a fleet seen off Kintyre which, 'I hope tis the regiments from Ireland.'[20] The Dutch government had been asked to supply 6,000 men, as stipulated in the Treaty of Guarantee for preserving the Protestant succession, but this movement of troops would take time, and both Cockburn and Argyll felt the threat was more immediate. In September, Cockburn wrote 'I'm weary writing bad news and good I have none, if the face of affairs don't change very you will not long hear from honest folks from this place.'[21] Their concerns were to be justified by the successful crossing of the Firth of Forth by Brigadier Mackintosh of Borlum, and his march towards Edinburgh.

William Mackintosh of Borlum was a colourful character who, the day before his trial for high treason, escaped from Newgate prison while exercising in the prison yard. On 4 May 1716, he was described in the print of an advert offering a reward for his arrest as, 'a tall, raw boned man, about sixty, fair-complexioned, beetle browed, grey-eyed, speaking with a broad Scotch accent.'[22] An experienced officer who had been engaged in the service of James VII in France, he had shown his mettle in 1715 by marching with a troop of Mackintosh men on Inverness and proclaiming James VIII king at the Mercat Cross. Joined there by MacKenzies sent by the Earl of Seaforth, he then marched the clan regiment of Mackintosh to Perth, joining Mar on 5 October. The numbers of rebels in Perth was increasing steadily, but with no sign of King James VIII, some sort of action was needed to keep the momentum going, and ultimately to join up with rebels in the south. A move was therefore suggested, but as Argyll was secure in his position in Stirling, which included the bridge over the River Forth, an alternative route south was required. Mar made a decision to have a detachment of their forces cross the Firth of Forth using a collection of small boats from the villages in the east coast of Fife. Diversionary tactics would be employed to encourage the government's ships down to Burntisland and also by Mar leading a feigned march of the army out of Perth and towards Dunblane to divert the Duke of Argyll.

In total about 2,500 men were involved in the diversion and crossing, which included a battalion of 250 men led by Lord Charles Murray. The boats left the east coast harbours on the nights of the 11 and 12 October and, though they didn't all make it across, it was an impressive military operation with only one boatload of forty captured. Those who didn't make it to the shore returned eventually to Perth. This relative success, however, was marred by the fact they had been given no clear instructions about what to do next. After a brief stay in Haddington and Tranent, Mackintosh led the rebels towards Edinburgh on 14 October, instilling a measure of panic there. Whether he had orders to march on Edinburgh or not is unclear, as Mar later described in a letter to Lord Kenmure, the leader of the Lowland rebels, that this move was a mistake. Chosen by Mar as the only noble in the area capable of leading forces for the Jacobites, William Gordon, Viscount Kenmure, was one of several leaders with no military experience, who reluctantly took on a role he was ill-equipped for, being, 'too calm and mild to be qualified for such a post',[23] but for which he would ultimately lose his life. As he was made general of the forces while in Scotland, the command of his troops had been given to Basil Hamilton of Baldoon, cousin of the Murray brothers.

In Edinburgh a message was sent by John Campbell, the Lord Provost, to Argyll, who was now in a very precarious situation. Aware that Mar was mobilising his force to move from Perth, Argyll's resources were stretched to the limit. Conscious that the loss of the capital city would be a disaster, he immediately sent 300 dragoons and 200 foot soldiers to Edinburgh, covering the approximately thirty-five miles himself to arrive on the evening of 14 October.

With no appearance of local support or instructions to take Edinburgh, Mackintosh had instead headed for Leith, where the rebels took possession of the Old Citadel. When Argyll arrived he soon realised it would be futile to attempt an attack on them and retreated instead, returning to Edinburgh. Mackintosh received orders from Mar not to advance further westwards and he also retreated, to Seton House. Argyll, then receiving the news from General Whetham that the rebels were on the march from Perth, made the decision that Edinburgh was now safe enough to leave and returned to Stirling. The rebels did reach Dunblane, but aware of Argyll's return and the possible arrival of reinforcements, Mar decided they had done what was needed and again returned to Perth sending Borlum instruction to head to the borders to meet up with lowland Jacobites and the Northumberland forces, led by Thomas Forster.

MP for Northumberland since 1708, Forster had no military experience but was given prominence in this rising due to the significance of his constituency, i.e the ability to disrupt the supply of coal to London, known Catholic support in the area, a possible landing for James VIII and supplies from France as well as the fact he himself was Protestant. He was one of six MPs whose arrest was ordered in London and so made his way home to avoid this, joined Lord Derwentwater and proclaimed James VIII king at Warkworth in Northumberland. James Radcliffe, 3rd Earl of Derwentwater, was a cousin of James VIII through his mother and had spent some time at the court of St Germain. Roman Catholic, aged 26 and recently married, he had a considerable, wealthy estate and was very popular among both his tenants and peers. Although joined by his brother Charles Radcliffe, the hoped-for support of large numbers of locals didn't materialise; avoiding an engagement with government troops under Carpenter at Newcastle, they instead made their way to Kelso to join the Scottish forces there.

At Kelso on 24 October, with a force of about 2,000 men, James was declared king and Mar's manifesto was read out, including the statement:

The late unhappy Union, which was brought about by the mistaken notions of some and the ruinous and selfish designs of others, has prov'd so far from lessening and healing the differences betwixt his Majesty's subjects of Scotland and England, that it has widened and increased them and it appears by experience so inconsistent with the rights. privileges and interests of is and our good neighbours and fellow-subjects of England that the continuance of it must inevitably ruin us and hurt them.[24]

After which, the people with loud acclamation shouted 'No union! No Malt, No Salt-tax.'[25]

With no direct instructions, however, the leaders couldn't agree on what was the best course of action to take next. They argued among themselves over different proposals, with the added issue of both the English and Scottish soldiers being reluctant to march into the each other's country. A plan to march to Dumfries, Ayr and Glasgow, gaining control of nearly all of Scotland, and then attack Argyll from both sides, was turned down as being too concentrated on Scotland. An alternative proposal to attack Carpenter's weak forces and gain a much-needed victory was also rejected. General George Carpenter, in charge of government forces in northern England, had set out from London on 15 October with instructions to go in pursuit of the rebels., His forces, however, included two recently raised and barely trained troops. As Britain had been at peace since the Treaty of Utrecht in 1713, the government forces were well below full strength and full regiments of infantry and dragoons competent enough to deploy to various regions wouldn't happen overnight. Borlum had supported the idea that the Jacobites should take the opportunity to attack, but Foster was reluctant to face Carpenter.

Included in the numbers that went south was Lord Charles Murray, and in a letter he wrote to his brother James he mentioned the disagreement among the leaders:

The Brigadier wanted to halt near Newcastle to get at Carpenter at once, but was persuaded by us to push on. We do want money badly, because we have little to pay the men with, who have twice proved themselves unruly, but we think that all things will go well now.[26]

Frustratingly, this letter is only published in one book and has no reference. Thanking him for sending money, it clearly implies the loyal Hanovarian brother James was giving aid to his errant sibling which casts a very different light on his loyalties.

Eventually, after some persuasion and the promise of support and supplies from contacts in Lancashire, the decision was made to march south, though 500 Scottish soldiers refused to go. When they reached Brampton, a small market town between Hexham and Carlisle, Forster received a letter, from the Earl of Mar, containing his commission as General.

Chapter 12

Preston

Lord Charles Murray commanded the Fifth Regiment with Lord Nairne's son (his cousin) as his lieutenant colonel. 'Charles ... appears to have been one of the Highland officers who distinguished himself by assimilating his manners to those of the clan or regiment he commanded.'[1] Patten described him as,

... brave and highly graceful, having formerly been a cornet of Horse beyond sea and gained a might good character for his bravery, even temper and graceful deportment. Upon all marches he could never could be prevailed upon to ride at the head of his regiment but went in Highland dress on foot, in his highland dress without breeches: he would scarce accept of a horse to cross the rivers which his men in that season of the year forded above mid-thigh deep in water. This powerfully gained him the affection of his men; besides his courage and behaviour at a barrier where his majesty's forces made a bold attack was singularly brave.[2]

The Jacobites advanced via Penrith, Appleby, Kendal, Kirby Lonsdale and Lancaster, entering every town unopposed. However, the majority of new recruits they received were mostly papists which, according to Patten, made the Scots very uneasy, as they had been expecting High Church Tories to join them. Robert Patten, originally a minister in the Jacobite camp, was later taken prisoner and turned king's evidence. He wrote a detailed first-hand account of the events in which he praised the 'prudent management and unshaken bravery' of his formers captors, but also paints a fair picture of his former comrades. At this point, however, he reflected that these supporters, the Tories, 'do not care for venturing their carcasses any further than the tavern' and quoted Forster as saying, 'from time to come he would never again believe a drunken Tory'.[3] On 9 November, the army left Lancaster to head for Preston.

Preston was a major market town on the north-west coast of England, which would also feature in the '45 rebellion. At this point it had a population of about 6,000, and possessed some quality buildings, including residences of both the Duke of Hamilton and Lord Derby, both of whom were relatives of the Murray brothers. In preparation for the advancing Jacobite forces, General Wills, who commanded the government troops in Cheshire, had contacted Sir Henry Houghton, the Whig MP for Preston and Deputy Lieutenant of Lancashire and Colonel of Militia. He had advised him to encourage the Presbyterian congregations in the town, who were considered to be more reliable than the large number of Tory or Roman Catholics in the area, to give aid to the government during this crisis. Houghton made some attempt at preparations, including retrieving cannon from a ship on the river and moving troops, but despite his efforts, the rebels arrived in Preston with no opposition. By 10 November 1715, the whole rebel army had arrived in the town and marched to the market place where, to the sound of trumpets, James III was proclaimed king. The men were then billeted and quartered in every part of the town.

The king's forces weren't far behind, however, and although Forster had been repeatedly warned of their near approach, he ignored the warnings and did nothing about making preparations to check their advance. Instead, he was preparing to march to Manchester when he was utterly surprised at being told on 11 November that General Wills was advancing towards Preston from Wigan. It wasn't till Wills was seen approaching the direction of Walton-le-Dale, near the Ribble Bridge, that any action was taken. Then, Lieutenant Colonel John Farquharson of Invercauld was sent to defend it, but as Forster went on ahead to reconnoitre, he saw the vanguard of the king's dragoons advancing and decided to return to the town another way, also ordering Farquharson to retreat as well. This was seen later as a critical mistake.

Due to his experience, it was assumed by the rebel army, especially the Scottish element, that Brigadier Mackintosh would be called on to react to the current situation. He was reluctant to lead the rebels into an area of open field combat, as he didn't think they had either the discipline or the experience to carry out the manoeuvres necessary for such a battle. He also knew that his band of soldiers would be at a disadvantage against horse and cannon which meant that, in his opinion, there was a clear advantage to the rebels to bring the battle as near to the town as possible, where barricades could be used to protect them while they could attack Wills' troops as they entered.

Finding the Ribble Bridge pass undefended, Wills crossed it and proceeded towards some fields higher up from the town. His intention was to stop the rebels' retreat, and for this he decided on two attacks being made, the first on the avenue which leads to Wigan, led by Brigadier Honeywood and the second on the avenue which leads to Lancaster, by Brigadier Dormer and Munden. They were under orders to gain possession of the ends of the town, set the houses on fire and stop rebels escaping. These tactics were later exposed as inadequate by General Carpenter, and underestimated the ability of the rebel soldiers.

The insurgents, meanwhile, positioned themselves in the town, setting up four main barricades. The first, under Brigadier Mackintosh, posted on the north and south side of the church, the second was on the outside of a hedge which flanked a broadway from Sir Henry Houghton's garden. Patten says this was at the end of a lane leading to the fields and was placed under the care of Lord Charles Murray. The third, the Windmill barrier, under Colonel Mackintosh and the fourth in Fishergate/Watergate under Major Miller and Mr Douglas. Finally, the The Gentlemen Volunteers were drawn up in the churchyard, under the command of the Earl of Derwentwater, Viscount Kenmure and Earls Wintoun and Nithsdale. Captain Wogan was posted with an advance party on a street a little above Sir Henry Houghton's house, and the rest of the men were put in reserve in the market place.

The initial attack was at 2 pm by Brigadier Honeywood's dragoons on the Churchgate barrier defended by Brigadier Mackintosh. After a botched first attempt at fire using two ship guns, the rebels managed to stop the advance of the government regiment, and forced them to retire with significant losses (both fatal and wounded) while, despite a major dispute between Mackintosh and Forster, the Highlanders had suffered little.

The government troops then moved on to occupy the houses of Sir Henry Houghton and opposite that of Mr Ayres, both prominent buildings. Lofty and overlooking the whole town Houghton's house had originally been in the possession of the Highlanders, but they had been removed, a decision which was later considered another critical mistake, and for which both Mackintosh and Forster were blamed. An officer in the service of the Earl of Derwentwater had been sent by the earl to the top of the church steeple to view the enemy's position, and he narrated what happened next. He observed an enemy regiment possess both houses, march through Sir Henry's garden and draw up in battalion at the foot of Broad Lane. The officer's advice was that,

> the Earl of Derwentwater close the right of his men to the range of houses that runs from Sir Henry's house to a street northward from the church, which was done. I gave likewise a signal intimating that the enemy was within the flank of Lord Charles Murray's men upon which the brave and undaunted Earl wheeled his gentlemen to the right covering the head of the Back land and receive the enemy with a very brisk and successful fire. Lord Charles Murray flanked them with as close a fire, and put them in great confusion and to flight. They sheltered themselves in Henry Houghton's house. I desired that the said house should be demolished by two pieces of cannon that were ready charged on the front of the churchyard and that the Earl and Lord Charles Murray should jointly attack the enemy without the town. I went for orders to General Forster who would by no means allow it saying that the body of the town was the security of the army.[4]

This attack on the barrier commanded by Charles was also narrated by Patten, who was with him: 'He behaved very gallantly, but being very vigorously attacked, wanted men and ordered Patten to acquaint the Earl of Derwentwater therewith, who immediately sent back Patten with fifty Gentleman Volunteers from the church yard to reinforce him who came in very good season.'[5] Having been sent to view the king's forces he returned to give Lord Charles an account,

> that by what he saw they were resolved to attack him again; whereupon Lord Charles gave orders to his men to be ready to receive them; and accordingly they came on very furiously. And though the King's forces that made the attack were for the most part raw new listed men and seemed unwilling to fight yet the bravery and good conduct of experienced officers much supplied that defect. However Lord Charles Murray maintained the post and obliged them to retreat with loss nor had they been all old soldiers could they have beaten Lord Charles from that barrier which was very strong.[6]

Charles was reported by another witness to have 'showed undaunted courage and killed several with his own hand.'[7]

The next attack was in the Lancaster lane, by Munden (whose troops remained on horseback) and Dormer on the Windmill barrier, defended by the Mackintoshes under the command of Colonel Mackintosh. The colonel and his clan behaved very bravely 'and made a dreadful fire upon the King's forces killing many on the spot, and obliging them to make a retreat.'[8] Again, the government forces suffered in this affair.

Night followed, and though there were still occasional shots fired, the attacks stopped. General Wills ordered lights to be shown in all houses of which they had gained possession, but this instruction backfired, as it gave the rebels something to fire at. Orders were then given to extinguish the lights, but were heard incorrectly, so that instead more were lit, which amused both sides.[9] The stated numbers of men killed and wounded can only be viewed with some suspicion, but it is safe to say that at this stage the number was far greater on the side of the king's forces than on the rebels. Patten says seventeen rebels were killed and twenty-five wounded, English figures are very hard to pin down but were thought to be 130–200. Despite the fact that the two main houses had been taken by the king's forces and the highest number of Jacobite losses were inflicted from this, Brigadier

Mackintosh felt that the day had gone well and was satisfied with their position. Even Patten admitted that at this point 'The rebels seemed to have had some advantage having repulsed the king's forces in all their attacks and maintained their posts.'[10] Mackintosh wrote to Mar early the next morning, expressing hope of a victory that day over General Wills.

The next day was Sunday 13 November, when the tables were turned radically as General Carpenter arrived with three regiments of dragoons. He had received an express from Sir Henry Houghton of what had happened and had hurried from Newcastle to get there in time. Although on his arrival he initially praised Will's efforts, he quickly saw the flaws in his tactics and rearranged some of the men, including putting troops at the Fishergate avenue, where rebels had been escaping. The balance was now tipped strongly in the favour of the government forces, as the rebels were completely surrounded.

Many of the Jacobites, once they heard of the king's troops' movements, realised they were now cut off from escape, and concerned they were also running out of powder for their guns, wanted an all-out attack on the enemy, dying as men of honour, sword in hand. But Forster, at the earnest persuasion of a chosen few, including Colonel Oxburgh and Lord Widdrington, decided to seek the best terms he could with the two generals and ultimately to treat for a surrender. Oxburgh had been a soldier serving in France and it was his counsel Forster had sought most when making decisions, but he was thought by many to have the character more suitable to a priest than a field officer. Widdrington, though also from a family noted for its bravery, was considered weak and cautious. When word reached the rebel soldiers of what was happening, there was a great disturbance between the men with the Highlanders in particular refusing to surrender under any terms. Derwentwater, Lord Charles, Lord Nairne, Major Nairne, Lockhart and Basil Hamilton were all reported to have felt betrayed.[11]

After the initial attempt at negotiation by Oxburgh, Wills stated that he couldn't make terms with rebels and they would have to rely on the mercy of the king. The Jacobite leaders were then given more time to surrender as long as no more barricades were built, and no one tried to escape. But about six or seven men did try and were cut down, so new terms were demanded by Wills in the form of two hostages. After much discussion, the Earl of Derwentwater and Colonel Mackintosh eventually agreed to go. But discord among the rebels increased as they realised Wills was determined to offer no favourable terms, committing to no guarantees at all. At one point, Forster's life was threatened by a 'Mr Murray' who attempted to shoot him, but was stopped by Patten. Later, a Jacobite prisoner wrote of his experience in the rebellion saying, 'I believe this is the first instance of a victorious army after action, yielding themselves prisoners to the vanquished.'[12] During the night of 13 November, some Jacobites threatened to make their escape but Brigadier Mackintosh insisted it was too late and much blood would be spilled, including that of the hostages. The next day the Jacobites accepted terms of surrender.

Both parties met in the market place where the rebels were to surrender their arms. The two Generals entered the town at the head of their troops, with the sound of trumpet and the beat of drums. The rebel Lords, officers and gentlemen volunteers were placed under guard in the houses and inns, Scottish Lords being set under guard at the Sign of the Mitre, The White Bull and the Windmill, while the rest of the men were marched to the church where they were held for about a month, with the townspeople being obliged to find them bread and water. Later they were sent either to Chester, Lancaster or Liverpool to await their trials.

General Carpenter sent his troops to Wigan and then to their quarters, as there wasn't enough room in the town for all of them, leaving General Wills in charge of the prisoners. By this time the two Generals had fallen out, which was ascribed by some to their lessening of one another's actions in the affair, though others said it was due to a misunderstanding between them from earlier service together. Whatever the cause, it clearly festered and three months later, in February, one called the other out in a duel, reported in the press:

> There being a challenge betwixt Lieutenant General Wills and Major General Carpenter, a duel was to have been fought yesterday morning, Brigadier Honeywood was to be second to

the former and Colonel Churchill to the latter, but the news being carried to his Majesty a file of Musequeteers was sent and secured them and preventing their fighting.[13]

Colonel Nassau was sent to London with news of the surrender, but returned quickly to Preston with orders concerning the prisoners. As six of the rebel officers had previously been in the service of the government, Nassau was accompanied by a deputy from the Judge Advocate, bearing with him a commission for trial by court martial of the officers charged with desertion and taking up arms against King George. Officers charged were Major Nairn, son of Bailie Nairn of Edinburgh, formerly in Lord Mark Kerr's regiment; Captain Philip Lockhart, brother to George Lockhart Laird of Carnwarth, formerly in Lord Mark Kerr's regiment; Ensign Erskine, previously of Preston's regiment; Captain John Shaftoe, son of Edward Shaftoe, gentleman of Northumberland who had formerly served in Franks' regiment; Captain James Dalziel, brother to the Earl of Carnwath, previously Ensign to the Earl of Orkney, and Lord Charles Murray, son of the Duke of Atholl, who had previously served as Cornet to Lord Ross.

Chapter 13

Sheriffmuir

While the Jacobite forces headed south, the Duke of Argyll had returned to Stirling from Edinburgh and to heavy criticism from ministers in London and the press, as they assumed the rebels would have been dealt with quickly. Argyll felt vulnerable and unable to take any stronger action until he had more troops, and so developed a growing resentment towards his critics: 'I find that not only by private letters which some of my acquaintances here receive but by the publick prints that not only my conduct is found fault with but the most monstrous falsitys asserted to lay a foundation for finding fault with me,' he continued that, considering the resources he had, Stanhope should, 'reflect whether it is not more wonderful that we have not been beat out of the country than that we have not gaind ground on the enemy espetially when you are pleas'd to call to mind that I have not had the least assistance from the militia.'[1]

Meanwhile, Mar's forces were being reinforced by the arrival of more men and their followers from the north, including Huntly, Seaforth and MacDonald. By the beginning of November, the Jacobite numbers were at their strongest, with around 9,000 men encamped at Perth who were being regularly trained and were now ready to move. Criticised for his inaction at this time, Mar was waiting for news of the arrival of King James. Even in London the rumour was that, 'The rebels are waiting to hear from France, rumour has it that the king will embark in a few days and they make ready to receive him at Perth.'[2] He was no doubt also waiting to hear how the army marching south had progressed, and for news of Rob Roy, who was said to know the best routes across the Forth, before he moved south. Mar wrote to that effect from the now rebel-occupied home of the Duke of Atholl at Huntingtower to Lieutenant General Gordon at Auchterarder, saying:

I wonder what keeps Rob Roy from coming to Perth, as I ordered him. Pray send him there immediately, for I want very much to speak to him; and if there be no alarm from the enemy, I would have you to come to Perth to-morrow morning that I may concert some things with you as to our march.[3]

Unfortunately, however, the Jacobite cause had been affected by the recent untimely death of Louis XIV, depriving them of the crucial guarantee of French support, and James had been delayed by the usual bad weather that seemed to curse every Jacobite rising, particularly when it involved ships crossing the channel.

While waiting for the northern troops to arrive, Mar had concentrated on securing supplies and weapons. According to a report by David Walker, a Presbyterian minister in Leslie, Fife, 'The Marquis of Tullibardine and his brother Lord George Murray came at the head of three hundred or some more on Saturday last.'[4] He described how their men had searched the houses for arms but then proceeded to search the burial place of Lord Rothes, breaking into the coffin and piercing the corpses till the stench made them cover it again. 'This Lord George was eye witness to, I am heartily concerned that such persons, come of parents of such eminency, should have been guilty of such a piece of inhumanity.'[5]

Later, Mar also sent parties of his men out to collect 'cess', the local tax, and one of these was again led by George Murray who, as a result, didn't take part in the battle on 13 November:

the next thing that was done, was sending Lord George Murray to Dunfermline to leavie that cess, which those sent before had left undone; he had nothing but Highland foot under his command, and his regiment being weak, the Duke of Atholes vassals derserting home daylie, who, besides the naturell inconstancie of those people were distracted betuixt the father and sons.[6]

This passage by Sinclair contained the accusation that, 'As to the cess, he levied it very effectuallie and kept five hundred pound sterling for his own use.'[7] John, Master of Sinclair, had served in the army under

Marlborough, but after receiving a sentence of death at court martial for his involvement in the death of two fellow soldiers, had been forced to remain abroad until he received pardon in 1712. He played a significant role in the 1715 rebellion, but the memoir he wrote on it was highly critical of almost everyone involved, and particularly scathing towards Mar. At this time his relationship with George Murray was also strained, as at one point George had, 'thought fit to attack me, and said flatlie that I was doeing things that if his oun brother did so he'd call him traitor,' to which Sinclair had replied,

> … were I his brother, I'd take him and lash him and told him it was less his business that anie bodies to speak so for it would be hard is a lustie young fellow like him could not find ane ensigne's commission somnewhere for that was all that in realitie he risked and bid him beware of that was of talking to me, for he'd gain little at my hand.[8]

Ironically, in 1750, Sinclair married Lord George's daughter Amelia Murray and other than expressing some concern for her young age, this was not objected to by her father.

The Dutch troops promised to Argyll by the government had started to gather in Ostend at the end of October, and on 7 November the first detachments sailed to the Humber.[9] This, combined with his own troops becoming restless and the onset of more seasonal weather, meant a move by the rebels was needed. Mar called a council of war on 9 November and made the decision to advance towards Stirling on 11 November, holding a review of the troops at Auchterarder the following day, moving to Kinbuck, just outside of Dunblane, in the evening. Recent prevarication by Mar had worked to Argyll's advantage, as it had given him time to acquire more men and resources, but at between 3–4,000 his numbers were still much less than Mar's when, on receiving news that the rebels had marched, on 12 November he too led his men out of Stirling towards Dunblane, taking position on the high ground to the east of the town.

In the morning of the 13 November, the Jacobites formed up in to two lines to the east of Kinbuck. Tullibardine's men were in the second line, between, Panmure and Drummond. After a spirited speech by Mar, which was even praised by the ever-critical Sinclair, the decision was made to move and engage the enemy on Sheriffmuir. The advance was made by forming the lines into four columns to move, and then back again in position, a difficult move for even a highly trained army and one which caused confusion, with cavalry and infantry ending up in wrong positions. Argyll too had issues moving his troops whose progress was slow; his best troops led with the less trained in the rear, so that on both sides the left flank was not in position when the right attacked.

When General Gordon issued the order for the Jacobite right to attack, they used the charge they are most famous for. After firing their guns, they would drop to the ground while the return fire was delivered, then while the enemy reloaded, would run forward with sword, targe or the butt of their pistols, accompanied with war cries. For the enemy, the charge was a terrifying but effective tactic. On this occasion Allan MacDonald, Captain of Clanranald, was shot dead in the opening minutes, but Alexander MacDonnell of Glengarry took up the charge, shouting 'Revenge! Revenge! Today for revenge and tomorrow for mourning.'[10] It was a complete success for these Jacobites, 'not only in our view and before us turned their backs but the five squadrons of dragoons on their left commanded by General Witham, went to the right about and never lookt back till they had got near Dumbliane almost two miles from us.'[11]

It was a different story entirely on the other side of the battlefield, where Argyll's right flank had attacked the Jacobite left. After the confusion of the earlier manoeuvre, the Jacobite-left were without cavalry support while Argyll, able to use his cavalry to full effect, had ordered they outflank and charge the Jacobites while they were still forming up. Despite trying to rally, after several such charges by Argyll's troops the rebels fled, pursued to the Allan Water by Argyll, convinced he had won. General Wightman who had recently joined Argyll from Edinburgh gave an account of what happened as follows:

The enemy were Highlanders and as it is their custom gave us fire and a great many came up to our noses sword in hand; but the horse in our right with constant fire of the plattoons of foot soon put the left of their army to the rout the Duke of Agyle pursuing as he thought the main of their army which he drove before him above a mile and a half over a river.[12]

After being informed of what had happened in the rest of the battle, Argyll stopped his pursuit and joined up with Wightman, turning back to where Mar had also regrouped. A tense stand-off followed; Mar again had superior numbers and could well have finished the day off with a decisive final effort, but he chose to do nothing. Field Marshal James Keith suggested the reason was that after sending an officer to assess the situation Mar had assembled his leaders to make the decision. When he returned, the officer reported the numbers were equal and the decision was that because the Highlanders 'were extreamly fatigued, and had eat nothing in two days, being averse to it, it was resolved to keep the field of battle and to let the enemy retire unmolested.'[13] Keith was a loyal Jacobite, aged only 18 at the time, and was attainted for his role in 1715, but was to go on and play a major part in the rebellion of 1719,where he shared command with Tullibardine.

Initially, both sides claimed a victory at Sheriffmuir, but in fact, both lost. Mar had the larger force and should have made a move at the final stand-off, but Argyll had lost a significant number of his men, roughly a fifth of his total force[14] and as an experienced military commander, was aware it had been very badly managed. Despite receiving praise in the press and from ministers for his efforts and for a 'victory', Argyll was under no illusion. He had been unimpressed by what he had seen from his own troops,

> … that some of the troops behaved as ill as every any did in this world, which makes it the more wonderful that the day should have ended as it did. I have further accounts of the preparations of the rebels whose vigilance and furious zeal is inexpressible. In short my lord they are ten times more formidable that our friends in England ever believed.[15]

Argyll was emphatic that more action was needed if they were to extinguish the rebellion completely: 'it may prove fatal to the whole if there is not what one may properly call an army opposed to these people.'[16]

Mar had returned to Perth, where he had ordered thanksgiving sermons to be preached and a Te Deum sung in the church for a Signal Victory.[17] He had written immediately after the battle to the Governor of Perth, saying: 'I thought you would be anxious to know the fate of this day. We attacked the enemy on the end of the Sheriff Muir at 12 of the cloack this day on our right and centre and carry'd the day entirely …'.[18] But in reality, the feeling among the Jacobites was very different. The immediate effect of the battle was a high number of desertions. As was the custom in the Highlands, once the battle was over men returned to their home and, as winter was near, they felt they had done what was expected. Added to this was the number who had deserted to escape reprisals following an inconclusive battle, and those who had been forced out anyway and were looking for an escape as soon as the opportunity arose. Due to this, it is difficult to say how many Jacobites were actually killed on the day. Mar claimed only sixty but it is likely the figure was nearer 600, Argyll putting the number at around 500.[19]

In order to stop this haemorrhaging of troops, and to try to rally them again to their cause before the arrival of King James, Tullibardine issued a proclamation which not only summarised his motives, but also those he felt would directly affect the people of Atholl:

> Besides any who have a true regaird for their own happines or Reall Concern for the family of Atholl, can never lye by on this occasione nor associat themselves with a most unjust authority which as yett prevaills in England and aims at nothing more than the Rooting out of true hearted Scotch men, particularly in countenanceing the Barbarous murder of that great Patriot Duke Hamiltone in whom wee had all so much Concern, and also the base Simon Frazer, commonly called Beaufort, whose vile actiones cannot as yett be intirely forgott is now not a litle carressed by the Usurpers of Regall Authority. But if all these

indignities with the future dismall prospect be not enough to raise the Spirits of Atholl men, let them further consider that the Marques of Seaforth and Huntly's men are now again to be raised more Numerous than ever and brought through Atholl, and if it doe not immediately appear as is necessary for his majesty's Service, the Countrey will find itself in the most miserable Conditione without any true prospect of Redress …[20]

But then word reached Perth that Inverness had surrendered to a force of Frasers and Grants led by Lord Lovat, and as the devastating news of the defeat at Preston came through, so did a letter to William at Huntingtower from his father at Blair, with an order to surrender; his brother's life was in danger and if he didn't surrender, he would have his blood on his hands.

Chapter 14

Court Martial – Guilty Verdict

The Duke of Atholl heard of his son Charles' arrest from his contacts in Edinburgh and shortly afterwards a letter in Charles' own hand. General Wills had had the sense, or better judgement at least, despite his hard reputation, to realise that allowing Charles to write to his father would be a wise move. Since the day of the surrender, Charles and some others had been put under a more restrictive guard than initially, as they had tried to escape. Charles now realised his only hope of a reprieve lay in pleading with his father for help. Although written in his usual script, the handwriting in this letter shows the stress and anxiety he was under, well aware of the desperate situation he was in. It must have been particularly difficult for him knowing the last correspondence with his father had not exactly been positive.

> My Lord, I have had the misfortune to be taken here prisoner as a great many both of our country men and english are, but there are four of us who have been officers in the army & are under much stricker confinements then the other prisoners who have not served, for we have sentinels who are above in the roome with us, & we doe not doubt but we will be treated as deserters, & I will severely suffer as such if your Grace does not make use of your interest at court to save me, which I beg and hope you will. Genneral Wills who commands here & has taken us prisoners has been so kind as to allow me to write this & is pleased to promise to forward it to your Grace. I give my most humble duty to my Lady Duchess and am your Grace's most obedient and most dutiful son, C.Murray Preston 16th November.[1]

The duke must have been horrified, but his response was immediate. To Lord Townshend, Secretary of State for the North, he wrote:

My Lord – I have had accounts from Edinburgh that Lord Charles Murray was taken prisoner in Lancashire and was to be tried by a Court Martial. His crime is so very great that I have nothing to plead for him but the King's mercy and goodness, who if His Majestie will be graciously pleased to spare his life I hope in God he will shew his repentance to God and King in such a manner as to shew his sense of so great mercy. I have wrote more fully of this to the Earl of Nottingham I am not able to add more but begs your Lordship will be so good as to join his grace in interceding with his Majestie on behalf of my child which I shall always own as a very great and particular obligation done to me.[2]

A similar letter was sent to the Earl of Nottingham and also pleaded for 'the life of a child'.[3] This child was 24, and had recently accused his father of not feeding him.

The traditional image of an aristocratic, proud and haughty magnate, head of a family who ruled with a rod of iron crumbles at this stage, as the duke demonstrated his genuine love and concern for his son, despite what had been said or done in the past. Without hesitation he immediately begged for his son's life, using every contact he could to assist, writing to the two Lord Secretaries, Townshend and Nottingham, his brothers-in-law Orkney and Selkirk, and of course his mother-in-law Anne, pleading with her to use every means she could to help. Atholl then wrote, for the first time since he had joined the rising, to William who was at the family home at Huntingtower:

Son Tullibardine – Tho' in my last letter to you, when you begun your undutyfull cours in joining with the E:Mar I then wrote it should be the last letter, If you did not then follow my advice and commands and return to your duty, now considering the life of your brother Charles is in the greatest hazard … This has made me once again write to you, to conjure you to prevent this guilt of his blood and your own by immediately making your submission to the King and laying down arms, and leaving that part that you can not but now see will soon prove your own and brother George's ruine as wel as of Lord Charles … Doe it without the least delay, for one day's delay may be fattal to Charles, who, if he doe suffer, his blood wil be required both by God and men at your hands. I am, Your Father.[4]

From this letter it is clear that he held William responsible for the circumstances his sons were in. He was convinced that it was William who was the leader in their actions and blamed him for this critical situation. His approach was, as his father, to demand that William's duty as his son was to surrender, which would give the duke leverage to get Charles' release, the address and unusually blunt sign-off on his letter emphatically enforced this.

William's reply must have exasperated him:

Mr Lord – I'm apt to think Lord Charles never took oaths ... I hope his life will not be in greater danger than others of our countrimen that were taken with him, for whose sad misfortune I heartily lament; however it's a comfort there is yet of the family worthy to be sacrificed on no worse a cause than probable many of the former Christians and Heroes would have chierfully suffer'd in ... There are so many honourable and worthy Scotch men with whom Lord George and I are engaged that it can't be reasonablie expected wee shoud leave them, and meanly to shift for ourselves, tho' wee are very sensible of your Grace's kindess and goodness towards us.[5]

Worryingly, the letter the duke received from Earl of Orkney was very bleak, as he said he had done all he could, that though his majesty acknowledged all the service he, the duke, had done, and that he was sorry for his son, he couldn't distinguish him from the others and it was, 'thought officers who deserted should be made examples of'.[6]

The court martial sat in Preston on 28 November. Captain Dalziel was able to prove that he had 'thrown up' his commission before the rebellion and that the vacancy had been filled before he took up arms. By this defence he saved his life, was handed over to the civil authorities and agreed to transportation to the colonies in exchange for a pardon. It was a different verdict for the others.

Captain John Shaftoe claimed that he too had sold his commission, but a lawyer was found to be still collecting the salary on his behalf. Ensign John Erskine claimed to have been forced into the rebellion, but witnesses contradicted this.[7]

> Mr Nairn and Mr Lockhart denied they were guilty of desertion since they had no commission from, nor trust under, the present government; the regiment to which they belonged having been broken several years ago in Spain. And, though they had received half pay they looked on it as no more than a gratuity and reward for the hazards they had run and the fidelity they had shewn to their late mistress Queen Anne, of glorious memory, to whom they had been faithful servants.[8]

The defence of being half-pay officers was a contentious one. In London, the Lord High Chancellor William Cowper had some sympathy with the officers, arguing in the Privy Council that it would be better to try them under civil law, because if half-pay officers couldn't serve on a court martial board then they shouldn't be subject to its authority either:

> And it seems they are not singular in this opinion for, we are assured that when this affair was debated in the Privy council in London several of the Lords were of the opinion that these gentlemen could not be tried as deserters by a council of war but by the usual proper civil judicatories and not by the martial but by the common law of the land … But as the council, so the Court-Martial was of another mind, and had no regard to this defence. Whereupon these gentlemen added that they did not repent nor deny the part they acted for they had taken up arms to restore their lawful Prince to his crown and to redeem their country from the slavery to which it was reduced by the union; and if they had a thousand lives they would do it over again, though they were sure to have the same fate.[9]

Charles pleaded that before he entered into the rebellion he had made over his Commission of Cornet of Horse to a relative, and that he had never received any pay from, nor sworn allegiance to, the government of England. But he failed to bring forward evidence for this, and was condemned to be shot:

> When he was sensible he was going to die, being removed to the house of Mr Wingilby, with the other half pay officers, he kept a true decorum suitable to the nobleness of his mind and the bravery of his soul and no unsuitable to the circumstances he was in.[10]

All five officers were found guilty; in an extraordinary move, however, Charles was given a month's reprieve. 'Lord Charles Murray ... was condemned to die for desertion. But, in regard to his defences and that he threw himself on King George's mercy, the council of war postponed his execution for a month; which we are told the Court of London is much offended at.'[11]

On 2 December, the four other officers found guilty were executed by firing squad:

> After this manner, with the greatest show of devotion the firmest resolution and the most Christian resignation, did they behave themselves from the first of their misfortunes till they paid their last debt to nature ... Major Nairn asked that he might not have his head covered and that he give the word of command but he was refused. After he was shot, Captain Lockhart and the other two officers laid him in his coffin, Lockhart performing the last offices. After him, Lockhart was shot and his body laid in a second coffin. Erskine and Shaftoe were then shot, and laid in a pit together without a coffin.[12]

Despite his being given a month's reprieve, Charles was not out of the woods yet and the news, although a relief, instigated another round of begging letters from the Murray and Hamilton families, relations and contacts.

On 13 December the duke received a letter from John Marshall, the duke's Falkland factor, in Edinburgh, saying he thought he should acquaint Atholl with some news, 'but I hope it shall be false and I hope the Earl of Orkney letter shall give your Grace better accountable.'[13] The note was from the *St James Evening Post* 6–8 December, stating: 'an order is gone down for executing the Lord Charles Murray'.

The news was false, but Orkney's letter didn't offer any more hope:

> … am sory to tell your Grace that I find the Government seems to be very angry at the Liberty the Court Martiall have taken, and these two last post days I have endeavour'd to know what was to be his fate, but can obtean noe answer ….indeed the publike papers of yesterday say orders are sent to put the sentence in executione, but I can not beleeve it, tho' I think him in the utmost danger. My mother has write to his Majesty concerning him, but if the Court Martiall and the gentlemen who have recommended him doe not succeed, its little probable any body else woud. I confess I think the merit your grace has to this Government deserves well the life of one son.[14]

A week later, Orkney was still not convinced of the safety of Charles' future:

> I think there can be no more done about Lord Charles for what the Counsel of War has done of themselves is strongest than all the recommendation could have been made by anybody, however I can't yet say what is to become of him for there no answer given about him but still it is some hope that I do not hear the sentence is put in execution but how it will go yet I do not know.[15]

Orkney's concern was also for his other nephew, Basil Hamilton, for whom he had better hopes of getting a reprieve, believing Anne could use her influence more in this case. Basil, the second son of his namesake who had died in 1701, had commanded a troop of horse under Forster at Preston, but he was only 19 years old and had never previously served in the army, or taken oaths to the government. Orkney felt that, as far as Mr. Basile I think your Grace may mack a very good argument of his youth he never took oaths to any government besides I think the merit your grace has to this Government and the cooperation that aught to be had to your Grace I hope may have some weight but then your Grace must express yourselfe so in any letter you write.[16]

The cooperation he refers to was the fact that George I had favoured George MacCartney, the man accused of killing the 4th Duke of Hamilton and, as such, it was felt a deal could be struck, a reprieve for Basil in return for MacCartney being allowed back in to English society. Orkney suggested Anne wrote to prominent ministers, the same ones Atholl wrote to, and that, 'Brother Selkirk should be sent up by your Grace for this very end and deliver these letters.'[17]

By this stage Lady Nairne had left for London to see both her husband, William, who had also been taken prisoner after Preston and Lord Charles. Atholl was to send his loyal son James to London as his representative, and to do what he could for the prisoners. At this point Atholl felt he would be serving the king better, as Lord Lieutenant of Perthshire by staying in Scotland:

My adherence to his Majesty's interest makes it at present impracticable for me to attend his Royal person, otherways I should have doen myself the honour to have waited in his majesty and most humbly begged on my knees the life of a son for whom I must own, I have nothing to pleade but his majesty's goodness and mercy which his Majesty will be graciously pleased to extend to Charles, that I shall endeavour to make up his and my other son's undutifulness and disloyalty to his Majesty by all the services to so merciful a king that is in my power.[18]

On the same day Mary Ross, Duchess of Atholl wrote for a second time to her father, Lord Ross, asking him to join Orkney and Earl of Derby in asking for a pardon. 'It will be the greatest favour you can do me and I can answere that the future of Lord Charles life will be suitable to so great a mercy.'[19]

Clearly still not convinced Charles was in the clear, Atholl again wrote to the two Lord Secretaries, his cousin Lord Derby, Selkirk and Anne, and again made every effort to get William and George to surrender. Via his brother, Edward Murray, he proposed that,

> the Marquess of Tullibardine, Glengary and Fraserdale, that each of them should write to his Grace, assuring him that they will leave the Earle of Mar and his party, and desiring of his grace that he will represent this to the Government … That it's probable the favour the King has shewen to Lord Charles Murray, the Marques his brother, in giving him a reprive for a moneth, is only to see if the Marques and Lord George can be reclaimed, and their still continuing obstinat may not only prove fatall to themselves but to him.[20]

However, the reply, again from William, was a refusal – unless the promise of indemnity include not only Charles and Lord Nairne, but 'all thos who wer taken with them in there regiments at Preston and also William Murray of Ochtertyre, with the Atholl prisoners taken at Sheriff Moor, may be fully included in the same conditions of indemnity as shall be agried on.'[21]

In December, instead of facing a firing squad, Charles was transferred to Chester Castle, one of many prisoners who were moved during a very severe winter when 'the snow lay a yard deep in the roads'.[22] Many prisoners were to die in the poor conditions in which they were held, and many were transported to the plantations in America.

Chapter 15

The King Arrives, Too Little Too late

T he weather for the winter of December 1715 to March 1716 was exceptionally bad, even for a period which is considered to have been experiencing a mini ice age. The Thames was frozen solid and 1715 became famous for the fairs held on it. But in Perthshire, where the River Tay also froze over, the effect was life-threatening for the local people. Living at subsistence level meant there were few reserves; it was very difficult to feed the people and impossible to feed the livestock upon which they were heavily reliant. As the bout of poor weather continued, there was a growing concern for all of finding enough food not only to feed soldiers, but also families at home and as a result, even more rebels deserted.

It was into this scene that King James eventually arrived at the end of December 1715. He immediately became ill and had to put off travelling until January 1716. Initially the news was welcomed in Perth, but rapidly soured when they realised he had arrived with no troops or supplies. A proclamation followed, announcing that his coronation in Scone was to take place on 23 January, but by that stage the rebels' prospects were looking worse than ever.

Throughout December, Argyll was making plans for an attack on Perth and expressed his concern at the problems following the Highlanders into the hills during the winter would bring, due to the terrain and the weather. However, he was also aware of deserting numbers in the rebels' force and was keen to be able to encourage this by offering clemency to those who surrendered, stating this would have more effect before the Pretender arrived. This approach was not welcomed in London though, which responded by sending General William Cadogan to ensure that an effective winter campaign was put into action. A highly experienced commander, General Cadogan had served under William III in Ireland originally, then saw active service in Flanders during the Nine Years War where he met the Duke of Marlborough, with whom he had a long professional career and close friendship, becoming known as being Marlborough's right-hand man throughout the War of the Spanish Succession. With his influence and skills, he was able to secure all necessary money, supplies and reinforcements for King George's army in Scotland, including Dutch and Swiss troops. Argyll, though appreciating the reinforcements, wasn't so pleased at the choice of Cadogan. Argyll had not got on with Marlborough, so was unlikely to see eye to eye with Cadogan. There was even some gossip at court of a threat of a duel between the two,[1] this was at the same time that Generals Carpenter and Wills were threatening each other! Argyll complained to Townshend that, as he understood it, in London the credit for the plan to attack Perth was being given to Cadogan, when in fact it was his plan.

The Jacobites in Perth were well aware of what was about to happen, i.e. that the government troops would march from Stirling to Perth with the intention of engaging them in battle. In the *Newcastle Courant* 9 Jan 1716, it was reported that:

> 'tis now said the Duke of Argyle and General Cadogan will not wait the arrival of the cannon and mortars etc from London but will march towards the enemy without loss of time and in the interim will be furnished with a train of artillery and other warlike stores from the Castle of Edinburgh.

To prevent this, or at least slow it down, King James was persuaded to give the order to burn the villages of Blackford, Auchterarder, and later Muthill, Crieff, Dalreoch (north of Dunning) and Dunning,

> … whereas it is absolutely necessary for our service and the publick safety that the enemy should be as much incommoded as possible especially on their march towards us … can by no means be better effected than by destroying all the corn and forage … and burning the houses and villages which may be necessary for quartering the enemy.[2] (26 January 1716, Scone)

24 January 1716, 500 clansmen, mainly composed of MacDonalds, Clanranalds, Locheill's, Appin's, Macleans, Glengarry's and Kepochs men commanded by Ranald McDonald, whose brother had been killed at Sheriffmuir, left Perth, heading first to Auchterarder. Guided by William Maitland, 200–300 of them then headed to Blackford, where Maitland's father was the innkeeper. They fed their horses at Maitland's Inn then went into the village, to the widow Jane Edie's house, 'one of the largest houses, in the middle of the town which was set on fire and being a lofted one with much wood in it was soon reduced to ashes.'[3] At the same time, a group went to the house of James Brice (a known Hanovarian) and burned it to the ground, they also set fire to the house of David Holmes and the house and shop of Alexander Gibson, a child of whose was found by a Jacobite lying in the snow. He took the child to the Maitland Inn and was heard to say 'that no King in Christendom would ever have a hand or be concerned in executing so cruell and barbarous an order.'[4] Only two houses are said to have survived: James Maitlands and James Davidson's, and those because the fires set were extinguished quickly after the rebels left.

Similar scenes took place in Muthill and Crieff, and in Dunning where they were led by Lord George Murray. He was accused of overseeing Highlanders, who initially helped the people retrieve their goods before their houses were set on fire, but then robbed them. Murray was said to have supped in minister William Reid's house, who had died a few hours before, but wouldn't keep it from being burned to shelter 'his sorrowful and mourning widow and children; yea they assert he said "that hew was sorry he got not the old dog's bones to birsle in the flames of the house."'[5] The story is reported differently in the Annals of Auchterarder however, where it is said they not only had time to remove 'their most valuable effects but yea, even to take out the flooring of their lofts.'[6]

All reports say it was done in a very unfair manner, with little warning and with the use of unnecessary violence, during particularly severe weather. No one would condone such an action, and George certainly doesn't come out of it well, but the contemporary reports were all written by the Presbyterian ministers whose interest it served to paint a picture of barbarian papist Jacobite Highlanders rampaging over the countryside. 'When I do reflect upon the maletreatment we mett with it does at once refresh my memory of all the instances of Popish cruelty I ever read of in history.'[7]

James himself realised that the decision was probably a mistake and did show remorse afterwards, asking that the money he left be spent on compensating the villagers.

> It is therefore our will and pleasure that all and sundry persons concerned do immediately prepare estimates of their several losses and sufferings and that they do deliver the same in writing to their several masters so as we may order relief and reparation to be made them for what losses and damages they have sustained in their houses, goods, furniture and corns or any other manner of way whatsoever.[8]

However, this was civil war and it wasn't an unusual tactic. Whenever generals saw a potential military advantage in inflicting destruction on economic and social infrastructure, they did not hesitate to do so; in May 1716, for example, several Jacobite houses in Fort William were burned.[9] Argyll confided to Lord Townshend, 'if they take the measures which I would do were I in their place it will prove a difficult task.'[10] He was implying that if the Jacobites took appropriately ruthless actions (the kind he himself would have taken), then attacking Perth would be very difficult. He was well aware that there was a lot of uncertainty and risk associated with a winter offensive, it was not the usual way to wage war as it was out of season and could easily have gone badly wrong.

Unfortunately, shock and awe isn't a modern invention; a scorched earth policy was used in many military campaigns throughout history. In recent memory and in the experience of many involved in this rebellion, particularly General Cadogan, was the devastation of Bavaria by Marlborough in 1704. The methods he used were solely to force the Elector of Bavaria into confronting the allies' army in battle: '372 towns, villages and farmhouses were said to have been laid to ashes … a shocking site', reported Captain Parker.[11] At least one victim, from

Auchterarder, didn't hold it against the Jacobites as he applied for a post with William when he returned from exile in 1745. Mentioning having suffered in the burnings, William Davidson stated that if given a post he, 'shall take share of any fortune and never leave you till death part us.'[12] It could be argued that this worked, as James and his followers got away without having to face the government troops. Argyll reached Perth on 2 February and immediately announced his intention to pursue the rebels who had successfully moved on.[13] When Argyll headed north, he was joined by James Murray who in the same month was, by Act of Parliament, made heir to his father Atholl's estate. On 4 February 1716, King James, with some of his leading Jacobites, took a ship back to France from Montrose.

A few days later the Duke of Atholl left Blair Castle and arrived in Perth on 9 February 1716, with a guard of 100 of his Highlanders. He was received at the Highgate Port by Colonel Reedings, Governor of Perth who had several of the canons fired in his honour, and the provost and magistrates who took him to the Town house, where he stayed for a couple of hours, before he headed off to Huntingtower.

Atholl had done his best to demonstrate his loyalty to King George, raising troops, informing Argyll of rebel movements – including that of his son Tullibardine gathering support at the end of October to join Seaforth on his move to Perth.[14] Atholl had also tried to persuade his sons to surrender and plead for mercy. But his actions had been limited while he was stuck at Blair and he didn't want to risk losing his strategically important ancestral home. Once he was back at Huntingtower however, the duke was far more active putting into effect a double strategy to save his son, Charles and other relatives, including his own brother Lord Nairne. First, he made every effort he could to be seen as the loyal and reliable supporter of the king, exercising his authority as Lieutenant of Perthshire, receiving submission of rebels, organising the tracking down of rebels and offering support to anyone sent from London to lead the suppression of the rebellion. Second, by continuing to write to his influential relatives and friends to get their support and help, and by sending his loyal son James to London to do all he could to help relatives who were imprisoned, there.

In March he entertained General Cadogan at Huntingtower, giving him the benefit of his local knowledge, and then left with him for Dunkeld. In his absence his wife, Duchess Mary, wrote to his son James about how ill he had been, suffering what seem to have been severe migraines. Clearly errant sons and proving loyalty were taking its toll. At least now the future seemed more promising as he had a much better relationship with Cadogan than he would ever have had with Argyll.

With the help of Cadogan the duke was instrumental in securing the submission and surrender of one of the leading Jacobites, Alexander MacDonnell of Glengarry, and this went some way to help further prove his loyalty to the crown. Lord Townshend wrote to Atholl, saying:

> I am to acknowledge honour of your Grace's letter of the 16th with the ... papers referred to in it which have been laid before the King who looks upon the intelligence given by Glengarry as very material and your Grace need not doubt but his Majesty will take a very great regard to what you have represented in relation to that gentleman. As his Majesty approves of the precaution your Grace took to acquaint Lieutenant General Cadogan with the contents of the letter Glengarry had received and to give out the orders of which your grace has sent up copies and which were at this juncture very necessary I have his majesty's orders to pay your grace his thanks for your great zeal and care in what relates to his service which I obey with great pleasure being yours Townshend.[15]

In a letter to Stanhope on 29 April, the duke praised the advances made by General Cadogan and described how Glengarry had surrendered to him, the duke, at Huntingtower:

> I dispatched an express ... with an account of the laird of Glengaries surrendering himself to me at this place and that I had sent him to Colonel Reading Governour at Perth where he has continued in custody in a private house in that town with a sentinel at the stair foot.[16]

This incident occurred less than two weeks before the duke's daughter, Susan, married Lord Haddo who became 2nd Earl of Aberdeen at Huntingtower. Susan was born there, so perhaps that was why it was chosen as the venue, but also the duke may have wanted to banish all hint of its recent rebellious associations by reaffirming his presence. His hard-earned position wasn't entirely without pain however; furious at the recent attention and accolades being expressed about him, Atholl had renewed his vitriol for his old adversary, Simon Fraser.

In September 1715 James Stewart, the Solicitor General, had expressed the opinion that on news he had heard from Inverness,

> ... it appears that his majesties loyal subjects in these part look upon the Lord Lovat's presence at this time of noe small consequence to his Majesties interest in that country. I know not well what to offer upon this head for he has been long abroad and I am a stranger to what his behaviour has been there.

He wasn't sure, in fact, whether to refer to him as Fraser or Lovat. Given the circumstances, however, in his opinion, they needed an ally in the Highlands and he should be offered the chance to prove himself, though Stewart was aware,

> ... there has been so much opposition made to him by the family of Athole that what may engage the one to his Majesty will disoblidge the other ..I am satisfied he might doe good service in that country at this time.[17]

With his usual guile and ingenuity, Fraser had returned from exile and promised to rally the Fraser clan for the crown, the Hanoverian one, in the hope of regaining his title. Alexander MacKenzie of Fraserdale (the husband of the younger Amelia Lovat) had marched for the Jacobites and though he had taken Frasers with him, they had been reluctant and soon returned when Simon Fraser reappeared on the scene. With the help of Clan Grant he successfully secured the surrender of Inverness, which in turn secured him a full pardon. He had taken the time to inform the government of the great services he had provided and asked that he be protected from the misrepresentation Atholl was spreading about him.[18]

Atholl was furious at this, and wrote to the Lord Justice Clerk, 18 May 1716:

> ... that your Lordship will endeavour to frustrate the greatest of villains Simon Frasers having any greater advantage then what the law will intitle him to who besides all his other bad qualifications is known to been a profest papist these twelve or fifteen years past and has never abjured that religion which makes it unaccountable as I think unsafe for any to have imployed him as a deputy Lieutenant as I heard for certainty both the Earl of Sutherland and Briggadier Grant have done.[19]

It appeared there would never be a time when the two would not antagonise the other because neither would back down and, in fact, used every opportunity to undermine each other. Atholl categorically refused to refer to Fraser as Lovat, as he declared he had no right to the title. Then, in 1717, Fraser fanned the flames of discord further when he got justices of the peace in Inverness-shire to make an affidavit concerning letters Atholl had written to some of the Fraserdale vassals during their argument years ago. Atholl wrote to Lord James on this subject, denying the accusations completely and saying: 'I think the best thing done with him were to send him to the plantations ... for he's certainly yet a papist and never renounced that religion which all ought to on accepting an office.'[20]

But while his hatred for Fraser, that 'villain of villains', never diminished, his anger towards his sons did and he was to show genuine concern for their welfare and future, despite being tested by further events.

Chapter 16

Charles at Chester Castle

The change of atmosphere in the city of Chester, brought about the by arrival of the prisoners from Preston, was recorded in the diary of Henry Prescott, the deputy Registrar of Chester Diocese. He wrote of the increased military presence and unwelcome violent incidents, which in his case helped encourage his own Jacobite leanings. Though a High Church Tory, he wasn't initially against the new Hanoverian government, but his allegiance changed over the months as he witnessed the treatment of the prisoners, punishments given out to soldiers guarding them, and through his association with friends who did have Jacobite sympathies.

On 29 December he recorded day three of the punishment of a soldier who had been caught drinking the Duke of Ormond's health. This duke had been stripped of his posts as Captain General, as Colonel of the 1st Regiment of Foot Guards and as Commander in Chief of the Forces by King George, and had been forced to flee to France due to his suspected involvement in plans for the rebellion in south-west England. Prescott tells how the soldier was bound to the post to be whipped again and 'bears the punishment without complaint or sense and when that is over his skin and flesh mangl'd on his back and ribbs to be miserable spectacle, hee is lett loose falls down and is with difficulty carry'd as dead to the guard.'[1] On another occasion, an 'unfortunate soldier who for a small sum of money was prevailed with to let two prisoners escape out of the castle, is shot.'[2] Prescott saw Charles in prison when he visited on a couple of occasions and was also to be a witness to his deteriorating behaviour.

On 28 January 1716, the *Newcastle Courant* reported that, 'tis said that the Lord Charles Murray, the youngest son of the Duke of Athol, condem'd by a Court Martial at Preston, for being in the Rebellion, has made his escape.' The head of the garrison at Chester did make a report stating that the prisoners daily attempt to make their escape during their exercise period,[3] and Charles had tried to escape in Preston, but no other mention is made of this incident.

The next few months were a particularly bad time for Charles. He had survived a court martial where his fellow officers had been shot, and would have heard of the recent trials and executions of Lords Derwentwater and Kenmure. He had fought alongside these men and couldn't fail to have been affected by their deaths. He was now confined in miserable conditions and entirely dependent on the father he had argued with to provide for him. Reports back home, via his aunt the Dowager Lady Lovat, also told of how he was ill with a fever, and how 'cruely he is used, to be laying on straw upon the flower, for they will not allow beds to be taken in to them and several others are sike in the same room with him.'[4] Prescott also reported on 7 February that, 'there are contagious and fatal distempers, fever flu and small pox spread among the prisoners in the castle.'[5] In addition to this physical suffering, it is highly likely that he suffered survivors guilt or post-traumatic stress disorder. His letters throughout his life show he was more emotional than his brothers, and reacted with greater sensitivity to his father's actions and the instability of his own situation. For the remainder of his life, Charles suffered frequent bouts of illness, described as a distemper. It is difficult to determine whether these episodes were a result of his fever and physical illness, or a more self-inflicted one, as is hinted by some members of his family referring to his drinking, most likely it was a combination of both.

The Duke of Atholl did have sympathy with his fate, and did his best to help him, applying early in 1719, for example, for more liberty for him, but Charles clearly also tried his patience more than his other sons. His brother James was given the job of looking out for him and constantly had to ask their father for more money, but as usual, the duke was in financial difficulties. He hadn't received recompense for the damage done to his properties during the rebellion, and his brother the Earl of Dunmore was threatening legal action for money owed. In reply to a request for assistance from James, Atholl wrote:

... as for Charles I must say considering how he has behaved to me he can not reasonably expect that assistance from me as if he had continued in his duty. And to tell the truth I can not send any more money than the fifty pounds which you drew on me with the twenty pound more which is not payed.[6]

In March the following year the story wasn't much different and the duke's patience was clearly running thin:

I must say Charles has less reason than any of my undutiful children to expect more money from me ... you know that he ought rather to apply to those whose advice he followed to break his trust to his prince and behave so ungratefully and undutifully to me.[7]

It's highly unlikely he meant this literally however, as he was trying to ensure Charles didn't mix with anyone who had Jacobite leanings.

Charles' future took a more positive turn in April 1717, when news reached Scotland that an indemnity was to be granted for those involved in the rebellion, which would give him his freedom. Atholl heard of this from Lady Nairne in London, whose husband, Lord Nairne, was to be included, but the duke was concerned that one of the few exceptions was to be his eldest son William. 'I got a letter from my Lady Nairne last post in which she tells me that she is informed that there is to be an indemnity soon and but very few exceptions and among those few my son Tullibardine is to be one.'[8]

The Act was passed in July, and included the release of 200 prisoners in Chester as well as those in the castles of Edinburgh and Stirling. In a pamphlet at the time, King George's clemency was declared 'not only great, but even extended father than that of God himself!'[9] It didn't, however, reverse attainders or restore forfeited estates.

The prisoners were allowed visitors and, probably due to the forthcoming indemnity, by April 1717 were given more freedom around this time, allowed to leave the castle as long as they returned by a certain hour. Under these conditions Charles had visited Henry Prescott's home where he was described as being 'very silent, not promotes nor joins in conversation, a grave, not morose, young Gentleman.'[10] During this period, Charles developed an attachment to Susan Bunbury, the eldest daughter of Sir Henry Bunbury, one of Henry Prescott friends and a known local Jacobite. Bunbury had lost his post as an Irish Revenue Commissioner in May 1715, having been found engaging in Jacobite correspondence and in possession of seditious pamphlets. This, no doubt, was the reason Charles' father and brother James were not willing to entertain the idea of a union between Charles and Susan, despite his apparently having fallen in love with her.

Charles had informed his family of his feelings by first writing to his stepmother, Duchess Mary, saying,

> ... the occasion of my writing this proceeds from a violent passion I have conceiv'd since a Prisoner for a daughter of Sir Henry Bunbury's ... I doe most earnestly beg and entreat of your grace not only to have your concent, but likewise you would prevail with my father to give his and to make the proposal now so that whenever I am at liberty I may from a most dismal confinement (which I most own I deserve) pass into a most aggriable one.[11]

Neither his brother James nor his father thought this a suitable match; James did all he could to dissuade him from pursuing it, but it appears Charles' own actions put a stop to it progressing any further when, during a visit to Susan's house, he refused to return to the castle and insisted instead that he was going to sleep in her bed. When she said she had no spare bed, 'he reply'd he would lie with her.'[12] At this Susan had broken from him, and ran to Prescott's house to spend the night there while a sergeant and four men were sent from the castle to carry Charles back where, 'he speaks a great many things very much out of the way; his looks are truly frightfull.'[13] Lord James and his father received news of this story from Charles' fellow prisoner Mr James Rose, who also wrote: 'I don't like to give the proper name to his distemper,' but he hints at it later by saying he had been sent word Charles was to pay him a visit to drink tea with him, 'tho I know he does not like it.'[14]

Henry Prescott also noted in his diary that at 12 on the night of the 8 April he had been, 'interrupted by Mrs Suzy and Bell Bunbury their hasty recourse to a sanctuary here from the odd pursuit of Lord Charles Murray.'[15] Hearing of this incident the duke's reply to his son James was that, 'I might not doe any thing to cross him or that might encreass his distemper, and I would gladly hope that either his too great passion for the gentlewoman or to much drinking might have putt him in the condition.'[16]

By 7 May Charles was reported to be recovering, James writing that a 'phisisiane that attended him writes to me that by proper applications such as bleeding and vommiting they soon got the better of his distemper.'[17] A couple of weeks later he wrote that Charles,

> ... continues to be very well and I hope given over thoughts of this affair, if he will be included in this indemnity as I am hopeful he will need money to pay what he owes at Chester and bring him from there ... his sickness has been a great expense to him and ... I should likewise be glade to have your Grace's directions how you would have him dispose of himself in case he be indemnified.[18]

The duke's advice was that he should return to straight Scotland and then go and spend some time with his sister.

Unfortunately, however, in June Charles had a relapse and, though James didn't want to give his father all the details, he had decided it was necessary someone look after him and had 'prevailed on Mr Gray' for this purpose, who was also to bring Charles to London when he was freed. James needed more money for this as he couldn't trust Charles, 'with any in the condition he was in, tho I knew he wanted it and has lived on credit these severall months.'[19] Hearing of 'the melancholy account of poor Charles'[20] although the duke approved of sending Mr Gray he was not happy at the idea of his going to London as he thought the distance (from Chester) was the same, but in London he would be further away from him and, 'I'm sure theirs as good advice to be had in Scotland as any places.'[21] Never keen on his sons spending too much time in London he expressed the same opinion in July that although he was leaving it for James to decide, he thought, 'London the most inproper place he can be in.'[22]

Over the next few months no further relapses were reported and in December, while at Dunkeld, Charles wrote to ask his father if he could be allowed to go to either Flanders or France to learn French. Unfortunately, a request for his uncle to act as guarantor of his actions abroad was turned down, and when Charles heard of this he – rather unfairly – blamed his father:

> I was in hopes to have prevailed with my Lord Selkirk to have taken the burden of me off your Grace but you have been pleased to write such a number of faults committed by me that I can not have the ashourance to importune him any more upon the subject, it is possible I might have undisceaved your Grace as to a great many of them if I had had an occasion to been heard, and when I was a prisoner and even before that of had it under your Graces own hand that all was forgiven and I was in hopes was likewise forgot.[23]

Although Selkirk hadn't been willing to comply with Charles' request, he did have some sympathy for him and suggested to Atholl that the best solution was for him to be sent to the King of Poland for military service, with a sum of £400 to help him make his fortune there, agreeing with the duke that sending him to a Protestant country was a better idea than him going to France. However, Selkirk did express a strong sense of caution to Atholl that immediate action was needed:

> I cannot help telling your Grace that if he is not helped at this time the bleame will be laid at your door that he has not made his fortune its no purpose to reproach this unfortunate youth with his past faults … he has behaved himself very well since his being here and seems very desirous of obliging all your Grace's commands and to submit to what you shall determine.[24]

Charles didn't go to France or Poland and didn't return to military service; instead he moved out of London to Itchingfield in Sussex with his father's blessing, and was given an annual allowance of £100 the same as his elder brother James. He lived with the Reverend Alexander Hay at the Parson's House. Hay and his elder brother were graduates from St Andrews University and had attended at the same time as the Duke of Atholl. The house was in the middle of a wood 'to which there was hardly any passable road,[25] and was recorded as being a refuge for attainted rebels after the 1715. Whether this included anyone other than Charles is not known, although a John McLean was buried there in 1724. Charles was clearly happier here and, at long last, wrote to his father expressing his gratitude: '...when my friends at London asked me if I had any security for my hunder pounds a year which your grace thinks fit to allow me ... I said I thought your Grace's word was enough for me.'[26]

Charles stayed at Itchingfield until he was taken seriously ill in August 1720 when he was moved to Knightsbridge for a change of air. The seriousness of this illness was reported to his father, and the duke was composing a reply to James via his secretary, Alexander Murray, saying, 'I give him my blissing & heartily forgive him of any undutifullness he fell into as to me, and pray God may forgive him whatever sins he has committed against him and grant him all happiness in the nixt world,'[27] when the news arrived that Charles had died. The duke's secretary finished the letter writing: 'His Grace is so much concerned that he could not write your Lordship but orders me to acquainte you that it is a great satisfaction to him to hear from your Lordship that he died so pleasantly and that you had a divine with him.'[28]

Chapter 17

Exile

W hile Lord James Murray, now the heir to the Atholl estates, was sent south to provide what assistance he could to his relatives held as prisoners in London, his father in Scotland was still keen to know the whereabouts of William and George. It was with some relief, therefore, that the duke reported to James he had received notice they had both boarded a ship to France.[1] With one son already in prison under threat of execution, Atholl may have felt he would have been pushing his luck to ask for a reprieve for the other two.

The threat to life for the leaders of the rising was a real one, Lords Derwentwater and Kenmure were both executed on Tower Hill in 1716 and the shock of this was expressed by Margaret Nairne, who herself was in London pleading for the life of her own husband. She described to her daughter how she had informed Nairne that the two lords were to die and he, 'showed more sorrow by far than ever he had done him for himself; and accordingly at ten these unfortunate gentlemen were carried to the scaffold in the sight of our windows and lost their heads.'[2] She went on to say that Lady Derwentwater, when told of her husband's death, had miscarried her child and become so ill that she was also expected to be die before the end of that day. Although she did survive this episode, sadly she was to die in exile of smallpox in 1723.

Both these men represented the key elements of the Jacobite leadership, Viscount Kenmure a Scottish Protestant, and the Earl of Derwentwater an English Catholic who was also a personal friend and relation of 'the Pretender'. For the government their deaths served a purpose because an example was needed, but ministers quickly realised there was now a danger of encouraging sympathy for the Jacobites and stirring up resentment by having further deaths. The dignity and courage shown on the scaffold, as well as the ingenuity demonstrated by the likes of Lady Nithsdale in rescuing her husband from the tower, could backfire on the crown, while a new policy of showing some clemency would be seen as admirable.

It wasn't in the government's interest to punish the whole of Scottish society, and the majority of families had had at least one relative involved. Many leading nobles in a position of influence lent assistance to their relatives who were now caught up in the aftermath, but they were also willing to help others who needed aid, knowing a future favour would then be owed in return. Writing to the Duke of Marlborough, Lady Nairne expressed this perfectly:

> No language, no words can express the infinite obligation this would lay on me, my twelve children, and five grandchildren to your Grace, as soon as they could speak … all of these shall be taught to bless your Grace and noble family and to pray God reward you for what all the services of or lives would not be able to repay.[3]

Wives and mothers played a significant role in this, pleading from the heart, for the lives of their errant sons and husbands. The power and effectiveness of this patronage owed a lot to the fact that the vast majority of Scottish aristocracy were still related to each other. The population of the country hadn't changed much over the previous fifty years, with the same small number of families holding the positions of high office. However, although Atholl did want James to plead the case of his uncle and brothers, he also advised he distance himself from his aunt Margaret, whose influence he now regretted, blaming her for, 'the ruine of my three sons.'[4] As the future 2nd Duke of Atholl, James now needed to be wary of his actions and allegiances.

After an initial forceful attempt to stamp government authority on Scotland led by Cadogan, using Dutch troops, by April 1716 he wanted to return south. The inaccessibility of many areas particularly in the highlands, the weather and simply not wanting to be there, all contributed. It also seems likely most rebels readily went through the motions of surrender in order to encourage his departure. Old and/or broken weapons were quickly given up, but no real account was made as to whether they tallied with what had been used or held during the rising. In some cases, including Atholl's, the Dutch troops had done more damage to loyal owners' properties than that of the Jacobites, and as a result their withdrawal was encouraged by everyone. For some time afterwards Atholl claimed expenses due to the destruction they caused at his property at Tullibardine, a situation which rankled with him given the loyalty he felt he had shown; he wrote to his son: 'I expect at least a thousand pound for plundering my house of Tullibardine by his Majesties forces and particularly my library…'[5]

In October 1716 the Dowager Duchess Anne died at her home in Hamilton, her son Charles Lord Selkirk by her side. Without doubt a significant figure among the Scottish elite, she had been instrumental in the lives of the Murray brothers, especially after the death of their mother. The fact that when in exile, William chose the title Mr Kateson (his mother being Katherine) and George was Mr Hamilton, acknowledges the influence of this family. Atholl had always recognised her worth and in a letter to James wrote: 'I don't doubt but you have heard of the good old Dutchess of Hamilton's death: she has been a great instrument of doing much good, particularly in the countrey where she lived and was much every way a most excellent person.'[6]

The duke himself continued in ill health after the rising and insisted on staying in Scotland rather than go south to demonstrate his loyalty personally to the king: 'lett his majesty know that my health is often so bad since the late troubles, especially since winter begun, that I am not in a condition yett to make so great a journey to London to wait on him.'[7] He was, however, constantly kept up to date with events from London and in April 1717 it was from Lady Nairne that he learned of the impending indemnity for those involved in the rising, but that one of the exceptions was to be his son William. Still referring to him as Tullibardine he wrote to James that, 'I desire you will speak to his uncle the Earl of Orkney or any other you think proper that have interest to make applications that he be not singularly worst used than others in his circumstances. I shall write to my Lord Orkney on this subject.'[8] However, a month later the duke had changed his mind and reported that,

... he seldon or never minded my advice ... I doe not think it fit for me to write to the king about him until he signifies his repentance for his crime against his Majesty and great undutifulness to me for it is too probably he would not accept of the benefit of an indemnity and then I might be blamed for asking a favour which he refuses.[9]

Perhaps he thought there was less chance of helping William as he had been attainted, but it is also possible that Atholl had already been alerted to the fact that William and George were still involved in fresh rebellious activity.

From the Court in Avignon, 28 January 1717, given by the Earl of Mar, on behalf of King James, William had been sent new orders:

To our Right and Trusty and Right well beloved cousine and counsellor, William Marquiss of Tullibardine, Lieutenant General of our Forces, Greeting.
... You are therefore to take upon you the said command of commander in chief of our said forces in Scotland in which we hereby empower you to grant commissions in our name to all officers in our said Kingdom ... to assemble our said forces and raise the Militia in our said Kingdom ...[10]

The result of this was to be William and George's involvement in the next Jacobite Rising of 1719.

As part of the continuing saga of the Wars of the Spanish Succession, Philip V had laid claim to Sicily and, sending ships there in 1718, he aimed to side-track the British government by supporting a Jacobite rebellion. Ships led by the Duke of Ormonde were to meet up with forces led by the Field Marshal James Keith, and Tullibardine in command and including Mackenzies, led by the Earl of Seaforth. But almost immediately the plan was hit by the usual Jacobite ill luck. The fleet led by Ormonde was wrecked by a storm, Keith and Tullibardine fell out over who was in command and most Scots were reluctant, since the Indemnity Act, to take a risk at rebellion again, many having accepted Hanoverian clemency.

A battle did take place at Glen Shiel, 10 June 1719. The Jacobite forces led by William included around 200 Spanish troops and consisted mainly of MacGregors (excluded from the Indemnity Act) MacKenzies, Camerons and Murrays led by his brother George. The government troops of a similar number (around 1,000) were led by General Wightman, who had fought at Sheriffmuir some carried with them for the first time coehorn mortars. Though fairly evenly matched the result was a defeat for the Jacobites, though the majority managed to escape while the Spaniards fought a rearguard action. Lord George's reputation hadn't come out of the 1715 Rising well, his main involvement being one of harassing the locals. He made a much more impressive show in 1719, however, as he led troops in the battle and suffered an injury to his leg. After the battle William spent some time in hiding in the Highlands, including the Isle of Harris,[11] eventually making it to France by the end of April 1720. George had also been in hiding but in different areas, including Inverness-shire Aberdeenshire, Forfar and Fife, eventually making his escape to Holland, landing at Rotterdam, on 30 April 1720.[12]

Both brothers found favour with James VIII who clearly genuinely liked them and appreciated their loyalty and support, with William continuing to be in regular contact with him. James wrote to William in June 1722 saying: 'I am extream sensible ... of your Constant zeal for all that relates to my service, and you may be assured of ever receiving from me all those returns of friendship and kindness which you so justly deserve ... James R.'[13] However, as with many exiles, both brothers struggled financially.

In France in 1723 George was visited by his cousin the 5th Duke of Hamilton who, in sympathy for his strained financial situation, had advanced him money for which he expected to be reimbursed by George's father. Initially Atholl had refused unless he heard from George that, 'he came to a sence of his undutifullness to me and acknowledge so much by a letter to me.'[14] By this time it was clear George wanted to return home and could only do this by accepting his father's wishes. He first asked permission from King James who replied: 'Since your father is desirous that you should return home I think you cannot do better than comply with him, for I suppose he would not propose it to you were it not to your advantage.'[15] George wrote to his father and Atholl responded enthusiastically by immediately applying for a pardon to the court for him with the hope he would soon be able to return from exile.

During his exile George had been attending a military academy in Paris and owed money for his stay there.[16] He reached an agreement with his father over the debt, as he not only expected payment of this, but also an advance to enable his return – and had then requested money for William too:

> I dare say you are not ignorant of the state of my friend his affairs; if either by the same canall or any other you could think of sending him some releef, I should leave this country with infinitely the greater satisfaction seeing, him in a better condition. In the mean time I remain my Lord, your Grace's most Dutifull, and most obedient son G. Murray.[17]

This issue wasn't to be resolved that quickly and still, in January 1724, Atholl was requesting the Duke of Roxburghe to, 'allow Lord James to putt your Grace in mind of what I formerly entreated to lay before his Majesty in relation to myself and also his Majesty's gracious pardon to Lord George Murray.'[18] In February the request was referred to a committee of council. However, despite having had no word of a pardon, in August George made the decision to make the journey home as he had got word the duke's health was failing. George sailed from Holland on 12 August 1724 and arrived at Huntingtower on 22 August to make his peace with his father and ask his forgiveness in person. Despite there being no pardon till November the following year, his decision to return home was the right one because on 14 November 1724 the Duke of Atholl died.

Aware he was approaching the end of his life, the duke had time to prepare and write his will:

> It is appointed for all men to dye and after death to come to Judgement, and when it shall please the Almighty God to call me from this valley of tears, I trust through the merits and

intercessions of my blessed saviour that my soul shall be carried by his angels to life and joys eternal.[19]

His funeral took place on 3 December 1724 when his corpse was carried from Huntingtower to Dunkeld Cathedral, under a pall of black velvet. The procession included his friends and family, a herald, several ushers, the Collar of the order of St Andrew on a black velvet cushion being carried by a cadet of the family and the ducal coronet being carried.[20] His last instructions included giving £100 to the poor of the parishes of Dunkeld, Logierait and Blair Atholl and £600 to be spent on buying books of Practical Divinity, 'which books are to be distribute at our funeral.'[21]

After receiving his pardon George was able to take up his new life at Tullibardine, accepting the terms of a lease for it from his brother James, the new Duke of Atholl. In 1728 his life there improved considerably after he married Amelia Murray, the only daughter of the deceased James Murray of Glencarse and his wife Lady Strowan. Amelia's mother had not been in favour of the match but was eventually won round by George who assured her he loved his wife and their marriage was to be a successful one:

> I acknowledge you might have cast your eys upon many who had advantages which I want, but given me leave to say it is no possible for any to have a greater affection and love for your daughter, & I assure you it shall be the constant study of my whole life to aprove myselfe worthy of her.[22]

In fact, in contrast to his brother the duke, for many years George's family life was a very happy one. When apart, George and Amelia corresponded frequently and honestly, with George beginning his letters: 'My Dearest Life …'. Their eldest son was educated at Eton, at the duke's expense, the intention being he would marry the duke's eldest daughter and inherit the family title and estates. In the event he was to marry the second daughter and become 3rd Duke of Atholl. They didn't escape tragedy completely, however, as in 1740 three of the children at home in Tullibardine were taken ill with smallpox, the youngest, William, dying aged 5. George wrote to his brother:

> I put the remains of my dear baby on Friday morning in the chaple. My wife and I take this occasion to ask the favoure of you that you will allow this Chaple to be the place of our internment [*sic*]. We are both sensible that it is a matter of great indifference where the body lys after death, but it pleases whilest in life to think of being laid near to those we love.[23]

It was a very different story for the exiled and attainted William, however, whose financial state rapidly declined. Many were aware of his desperate situation, the Countess of Panmure wrote to Lord George in 1725 hoping that the new duke, 'would act a kind part to Lord Tullibardine'.[24] But the allowance he did receive didn't stop him from going to prison for a short period for his debts. In 1731 William's friend Monsieur van Exaerde wrote:

> I have the honour to inform you that the Duke of Atholl is in the most serious embarrassment in the world on account of the necessary repairs which have been made in his house. The workmen will not finish without having money, they make him a scandal and an affront which bring him to shame ...[25]

He was helped out of this particular dire situation but throughout his exile he struggled to cope and in 1743 resorted to asking his brother for more assistance. In addition to his economic woes and no doubt compounded by them, William's health also began to deteriorate during this time, as he became severely affected by rheumatism.

Since the death of this father, William had been called 'the Duke of Atholl' by his friends and acquaintances in France and as such remained a significant figure in Jacobite circles, a status he retained throughout his life. It was no great surprise then that, despite his chronic financial state, he was called on to be one of the few men who would sail with Bonnie Prince Charlie in 1745.

I desire you would tell the Duke of Atholl that I should be glad to see him at Navare, having some thing to discorse with him; but I desire his coming may be kept a secret from all mortals without exception. It must be your business to provide for his journey, and I desire of him only to follow the directions he will receive from me by you. Charles P. (Paris 26 May 1745.)[26]

William's status was further re-enforced in Scotland when he was given the role of holding up the standard at Glenfinnan and reading the manifesto marking the start of the 1745 Rising.

The surprise instead was that George, his contented, happily married, family-man brother, should make the decision to join this rising knowing full well his future, and that of his beloved wife, would most likely be ruined. George explained his decision in a letter to his brother James:

I never did say to any person in life that I would not ingage in the cause I always in my heart thought just and right as well as for the interest, good, and liberty of my country.

But this letter is not wrote with a view to argue or reason with you upon the subject. I own frankly that now I am to ingage, that what I do may and will be reccon'd desperate and tho' all appearance seem to be against me, interest, prudence and the obligations to you which I ly under, would prevent most people in my situation from taking a resolution that may very probably end in my utter ruen.[27]

His decision to join the Jacobites in the '45 was crucial; he was to become an instrumental figure in the outcome of many of the major events of the rising, not least the decision to turn back at Derby.

Epilogue

ollowing the brothers' lives up to and during the rising of 1715, it is far from obvious that the future Jacobite general, the most famous of them all, would be Lord George. In 1715 he comes across as immature, wilful and headstrong, having the least military potential. It is, therefore, all the more remarkable that he did then become the man he did: a decisive, versatile, military strategist who was highly respected by his men, though not loved by his peers. He was to have a notoriously fractious relationship with Bonnie Prince Charlie, while the prince's father James III respected and welcomed him, even today Lord George is admired and criticised in equal measure. In 1715 he was still relatively young and had been indulged to some extent by his elder brothers and father who encouraged him to have a life away from the military. However, like his father and brothers he was proud, with a strong sense of duty to both his family and country. This family, who played such a fundamental role in Scottish history at this time, instilled in him high standards and admirable reputations which he emulated and that meant choosing the path he thought was right for his country and the king 'across the water', despite the detriment he knew would follow for him personally. 'My life, my fortune, my expectations, the happyness of my wife & children, are all at stake (& the chances are against me) & yet a principle of (what to me) Honour & Duty to King and Country, outweighs everything.'[1]

After the failure of the '45 George went into exile again, from which he never returned. While in exile he kept in touch with his king and was joined for many periods by his wife who, along with their daughter, were with him in 1760 when he died in Medemblik, Holland, after a short illness. William's fate was far more tragic. Taken prisoner after the defeat at Culloden, he was sent to prison in the Tower of London where he died of an infection in 1746 and was buried in the chapel there. Had he survived the illness it was more than likely he would have been found guilty at trial and executed. This was to be the fate of the Murray family arch-nemesis Simon Fraser, whose treachery and side-changing finally caught up with him in 1747 when, found guilty of treason, he was beheaded on Tower Hill.

The Murray brothers each played a significant role in the events of their time; reading through the letters and exploring their history, however, it becomes apparent that, as always, there was a strong, though less commonly credited influence on these men: the women. Throughout this period as mothers, grandmothers, wives and aunts, they were heavily involved, as well as consulted, respected, and in one case even blamed for events and decisions made. Often this was also of their own volition as many of these women demonstrated an active interest of their own in what was happening around them and a keenness to be involved. It becomes very clear that the Murray, Hamilton and Nairne ladies had a very meaningful impact on the lives of their men and while the brothers are the names recognised in history, their female relatives were also of crucial importance.

Notes

Introduction
1. NRAS332/C3/1719.
2. *Jacobite Songs and Ballads* (Selected) ed., with notes and Introductory note by G.S. MacQuoid 1887.

Chapter 1
1. National Library of Scotland Exhibition 'Game of Crowns' 2015.
2. *Early Travellers in Scotland* Peter Hume Brown (ed.)1891 – Thomas Morer A Short Account of Scotland published 1715.
3. A Selection from the Papers of Patrick Earl of Marchmont p.128.

Chapter 2
1. Chronicles of the Atholl and Tullibardine Families Vol II p.70.
2. The Lockhart Papers: Containing Memoirs and Commentaries upon the Affairs of Scotland from 1702 to 1715 by Geroge Lockhart, Esq. Of Carnwarth Vol 1. p.73.
3. *Memoirs of the Secret Services of John Macky* p.184.
4. Chronicles of the Atholl and Tullibardine Families Vol II p.130.
5. *A Social History of the Atholl Estates* Leah Leneman. p.152.
6. National Records of Scotland GD406/1/7960.
7. *A Social History of the Atholl Estates* Leah Leneman p.167.
8. R.K. Marshall Hamilton Katherine, Duchess of Atholl (1632–1707) *Oxford Dictionary of National Biography* article 70530.
9. NRS GD406/1/6064.
10. National Record Archives NRAS332/M/2/66.
11. Ibid.
12. Ibid.
13. Chronicles of the Atholl and Tullibardine Families Vol 1 p.310.
14. Ibid p.335.
15. *King William and the Scottish Politicians* P.W.J. Riley p.121.
16. State-Papers and Letters Addressed to William Carstares by J. MacCormick p.298.
17. Chronicles of the Atholl and Tullibardine Families Vol 1 p.446.
18. Ibid p.333.
19. Ibid p.332.

Chapter 3
1. Memoirs of the Life of Simon Lord Lovat written by himself. p.18.
2. Memoirs of the Life of Simon Lord Lovat written by himself. p.25.
3. Chronicles of the Atholl and Tullibardine Families Vol 1 p.375 – diemeted = resigned his commission of the company he had a captaincy in.
4. Memoirs of the Life of Simon Lord Lovat written by himself. p.26.
5. Ibid p.34.
6. Ibid.
7. Chronicles of the Atholl and Tullibardine Families Vol 1 p.389.
8. Memoirs of the Life of Simon Lord Lovat written by himself p.62.
9. Chronicles of the Atholl and Tullibardine Families Vol 1 p.401.
10. State Papers and Letters Addressed to William Carstares p.435.
11. *A Collection of Scarce and Valuable Tracts* Walter Scott 1814 Vol 12 pp.441–446.
12. Ibid.
13. Ibid.
14. Chronicles of the Atholl and Tullibardine Families Vol 1 p.401.
15. Papers of Patrick Earl of Marchmont p.143.
16. *A Collection of Scarce and Valuable Tracts* Walter Scott 1814 Vol 12 p.446.
17. Ibid p.437.
18. A Selection from the papers of the Earls of Marchmont Papers of Patrick p.170.
19. Chronicles of the Atholl and Tullibardine Families Vol 1 p.456.
20. NRS GD406/1/6641.
21. Ibid.
22. Ibid.
23. NRS GD406/1/6721.
24. NRS GD406/1/6722.
25. NRS GD406/1/6442.
26. Ibid.
27. NRS GD406/1/6672.
28. Chronicles of the Atholl and Tullibardine Families Vol 1 p.457.
29. Ibid p.421.
30. Ibid p.401.
31. Ibid p.420.
32. Ibid p.429.

Chapter 4
1. Chronicles of the Atholl and Tullibardine families Vol 1 p.506.
2. *The Records of the Parliaments of Scotland to 1707*, K.M. Brown et al eds. (St Andrews, 2007–18), 1704/7/7 http://www.rps.ac.uk/trans/1704/7/7.
3. Ibid trans/1704/7/68.
4. Memoirs of the Life of Lord Lovat p.171.

5. Ibid p.175.
6. Chronicles of the Atholl and Tullibardine Families Vol II P.39.
7. *Memoirs Concerning the Affairs of Scotland* George Lockhart p.72/3.
8. Blair Archives 45/6/88.
9. Ibid 45/6/ 94.
10. Ibid 45/6/121.
11. Ibid 45/6/125.
12. Chronicles of the Atholl and Tullibardine Families Vol II p.57.
13. Ibid.
14. Ibid p.58.
15. *Oxford Dictionary of National Biography* John R. Young.
16. *The Records of the Parliaments of Scotland to 1707*, K.M. Brown et al eds. (St Andrews, 2007–18), 1706/10/212.
17. Ibid.
18. Chronicles of the Atholl and Tullibardine Families Vol II p.70.
19. The Secret History of Colonel Hooke's Negotiations in Scotland in favour of the Pretender 1707 written by himself p.26 & 27.
20. Lockhart Papers Vol II p.231.
21. The Secret History of Colonel Hooke's Negotiations p.58.
22. Chronicles of the Atholl and Tullibardine Families Vol II p.87.
23. Chronicles of the Atholl and Tullibardine Families Vol 1 p.331.
24. Blair Archives 45/12/121.
25. Ibid Box 45/8/1.
26. *The Secret History of Colonel Hooke's Negotiations* p.57.
27. Chronicles of the Atholl and Tullibardine Families Vol II p.90.

Chapter 5
1. *The Days Of Duchess Anne* R. Marshall 1973 p.146.
2. Chronicles of the Atholl and Tullibardine Families Vol 1 p.501.
3. Ibid Vol 1 p.289.
4. Blair Archives 45/1/167.
5. Ibid 45/3/43.
6. Ibid 45/2/238.
7. *The Days Of Duchess Anne* R. Marshall 1973 p.146 & 147.
8. Chronicles of the Atholl and Tullibardine Families Vol 1 p.503.
9. Blair Archives 45/4/174.
10. Ibid 45/5/38.
11. Ibid.
12. Chronicles of the Atholl and Tullibardine Families Vol II p.67.
13. NRS GD406/1/8038.
14. Chronicles of the Atholl and Tullibardine Families Vol I p.466.
15. NRS GD406/1/7960.
16. Chronicles of the Atholl and Tullibardine Families Vol I p.462.

17. NRAS332/M/2/66.
18. Chronicles of the Atholl and Tullibardine Families Vol I p.426.
19. NRAS332/M/2/66.
20. *The Ladies of the Covenant: Memoirs of Distinguished Scottish Female Characters* p.589.
21. Chronicles of the Atholl and Tullibardine Families Vol II p.56 & 57.
22. Blair Archives 45/2/Sept.
23. *The Jacobite General* Katherine Tomasson p.1.
24. Blair Archives 45/3/169.
25. *The Ladies of the Covenant: Memoirs of Distinguished Scottish Female* Characters p.59.
26. NRAS332/M/2/66.
27. NRS GD406/1/6894.
28. Blair Archives 45/2/154.
29. Ibid 45/2/195.
30. Ibid 45/2/114.
31. Blair Archives 45/2/poem.
32. *The Ladies of the Covenant: Memoirs of Distinguished Scottish Female* Characters p.593.
33. NRS GD406/1/6378.
34. NRS GD406/1/6638.
35. Blair Archives 45/1/108.
36. Chronicles of the Atholl and Tullibardine Families Vol II p.69.
37. Ibid.

Chapter 6

1. *The Ladies of the Covenant: Memoirs of Distinguished Scottish Female* Characters p.146.
2. www.visionofbritain.org.uk/travellers/defoe/38.
3. Blair Archives 45/1/75.
4. Ibid 45/3/99.
5. *The Ladies of the Covenant: Memoirs of Distinguished Scottish Female Characters* p.177.
6. Blair Archives 45/3/34.
7. NRA/S332/C3/1719.
8. Chronicles of Atholl and Tullibardine Families Vol II p.115.
9. *Newcastle Courant* 8 February 1716.
10. *Diary of Mary Countess Cowper, Lady of the Bedchamber to the Princess of Wales, 1714–1720* p.109.
11. Blair Archives 45/10/158.
12. Chronicles of Atholl and Tullibardine Families Vol II p.145.
13. NRA S332/C3/1718.
14. Blair Archives 45/10/182.

15. *Newcastle Courant* 30 November 1712.
16. Chronicles of Atholl and Tullibardine Families Vol I p.478.
17. Ibid p.471.
18. Ibid p.473.
19. *Manuscripts of the Duke of Atholl* p.59.
20. NRS GD406/1/4350.
21. *The Scottish Nation: Biographical History of the People of Scotland* William Anderson Vol III.
22. Blair Archives 45/1/2 Oct.
23. A Bundle of Jacobite Letters S.H.R. Vol IV.
24. Chronicles of Atholl and Tullibardine Families Vol II p.41.
25. Ibid p.80.
26. Blair Archives 45/2/78.
27. *The Jacobite Lairds of Gask* Thomas Laurence Kington-Oliphant p.37.
28. Chronicles of Atholl and Tullibardine Families Vol II p.251.

Chapter 7
 1. Chronicles of Atholl and Tullibardine Families Vol I p. 373.
 2. NRS GD406/1/7960.
 3. Chronicles of Atholl and Tullibardine Families Vol I p. 475.
 4. Ibid p.484.
 5. Ibid Vol II p.54.
 6. Blair Archives 45/2/100.
 7. Ibid 45/2/April 21.
 8. Ibid 45/2/195.
 9. Ibid 45/2/215.
10. Ibid 45/3/60.
11. Ibid 45/3/29.
12. Ibid 45/4/15.
13. Ibid 45/4/22.
14. Ibid.
15. Chronicles of Atholl and Tullibardine Families Vol II p.21.
16. Ibid p.34.
17. Ibid p.43.
18. Blair Archives 45/5/11 P. here refers to her sister Margaret the Countess of Panmure who was the wife of James the 4th Earl, a committed Jacobite who was to play an active role in the 1715 rising.
19. Ibid 45/5/50.
20. Ibid 45/5/52.
21. Ibid 45/6/15.
22. Ibid 45/6/43.
23. Ibid.
24. Ibid 45/6/56 *the shortest madness is the best.

25. Chronicles of Atholl and Tullibardine Families Vol II p.54.
26. Ibid p.59.
27. *The Manuscripts of the Duke of Atholl* No. 155.
28. Chronicles of Atholl and Tullibardine Families Vol II p.66.
29. Ibid p.67.
30. Ibid p.72.
31. Blair Archives 45/6/91.
32. NRS GD406/1/10340.
33. Chronicles of Atholl and Tullibardine Families Vol II p.111.
34. Blair Archives 45/9/76.
35. Ibid 45/9/83.
36. Ibid 45/9/90.
37. Chronicles of Atholl and Tullibardine Families Vol II p.112.
38. Blair Archives 45/9/85.
39. Ibid 45/9/97.
40. Chronicles of Atholl and Tullibardine Families Vol II p.114.

Chapter 8

1. Chronicles of Atholl and Tullibardine Families Vol II p.49.
2. NRAS332/M/2/66.
3. NRAS332/M/2/66 1707.
4. Blair Archives 45/7/212.
5. Ibid.
6. Ibid.
7. Ibid 45/7/213.
8. NRAS332/M/2/66.
9. Ibid.
10. Ibid.
11. Chronicles of Atholl and Tullibardine Families Vol II p.114.
12. Blair Archives 45/9/103.
13. Ibid.
14. NRS GD112/39/252/9.
15. Chronicles of Atholl and Tullibardine Families Vol II p.136.
16. Ibid p.163.
17. Blair Archives 45/10/149.
18. Ibid 45/10/150.
19. Chronicles of Atholl and Tullibardine Families Vol V ADDENDA to Vol II p.135.
20. NRAS332/C3/1647.
21. Blair Archives 45/10/172.
22. Chronicles of Atholl and Tullibardine Families Vol II p.144.

Chapter 9

1. Chronicles of Atholl and Tullibardine Families Vol I p.169.
2. NRS GD406/1/7040.
3. *The History of Perth Academy* Edward Smart.
4. Chronicles of Atholl and Tullibardine Families Vol II p.118.
5. Ibid p.135.
6. NRS GD406/1/5805.
7. NRS GD406/1/7910.
8. NRS GD112/39/263/1.
9. Chronicles of Atholl and Tullibardine Families Vol II p.139.
10. Blair Archives 45/10/91.
11. Chronicles of Atholl and Tullibardine Families Vol II p.140.
12. Ibid p.147.
13. Ibid p.161.
14. Ibid p.149.
15. NRA2332/C3/1718.
16. Blair Archives 45/11/105.
17. Ibid 45/12/44.
18. Ibid 45/12/9.
19. Ibid.
20. NRAS332/C3/1721.
21. NRAS332/C3/1647.
22. Chronicles of Atholl and Tullibardine Families Vol II p.155.
23. NRAS332/C3/1717.
24. Blair Archives 45/11/198.
25. NRAS332/C3/1647.
26. NRA S332/C3/37.
27. NRAS332/C3/1653.
28. Blair Archives 45/11/90.
29. Ibid 45/11/158.
30. Ibid 45/11/163.
31. Ibid 45/11/173.
32. Ibid 45/11/178 The shortest folly is the best.
33. NRAS332/C3/1653.

Chapter 10

1. NRA S233/41/2866.
2. Blair Archives 45/11/147.
3. Ibid 45/11/148.
4. Ibid 45/11/150.
5. James Murray of Stormont to James III September 3 1715. Calendar of the Stuart papers belonging to his Majesty the King p.415.
6. NRAS332/C3/1721.

7. Blair Archives 45/11/154.
8. Ibid 45/11/167.
9. NRAS332/C3/1721.
10. Blair Archives 45/11/178.
11. NRA S332/C3/1724.
12. NRAS332/C3/1725.
13. Blair Archives 45/12/56.
14. NRAS332/C3/1726.
15. Ibid.
16. TNA SP54/7/56B.
17. Chronicles of Atholl and Tullibardine Families Vol II p.184.
18. Ibid p.183.
19. *The History of the Rebellion Rais'd Against his Majesty King George* Peter Rae.
20. Chronicles of Atholl and Tullibardine Families Vol II p.187.

Chapter 11

1. *The History of the Rebellion Rais'd Against his Majesty King George* Peter Rae p.135.
2. Ibid p.140.
3. Ibid p.151.
4. TNA SP35/1/30.
5. *Popular Protest in Early Hanoverian London* Nicholas Rogers.
6. *1715: The Story of the Rising* A & H Tayler p.197.
7. *Memoirs of the Insurrection In Scotland* John, Master of Sinclair p.58.
8. *Oxford Dictionary of National Biography* Erskine, John 6th Earl of Mar.
9. *1715: The Story of the Rising* A & H Tayler p.47.
10. NRA S332/C3/55.
11. Chronicles of Atholl and Tullibardine Families Vol II p.191.
12. *Memoirs of the Secret Services of John Mackay* p.190.
13. *Memoirs Concerning the Affairs of Scotland* Lockhart of Carnwath p.132–3.
14. Chronicles of Atholl and Tullibardine Families Vol II p.195.
15. *The Jacobite Lairds of Gask* T.L. Kington Oliphant p.30.
16. NRA S332/C3/55.
17. *1715: The Story of the Rising* A & H Tayler p.53.
18. Ibid p.52.
19. TNA SP54/8/89.
20. TNA SP54/7/24.
21. TNA SP54/8/77.
22. www.oxforddnb.com.
23. *The History of The Rebellion in the Year 1715* Robert Patten p.39.
24. Ibid p.33.
25. Ibid p.37.
26. *Historical Notes; or, Essays on '15 and '45* D. Murray p.83.

Chapter 12

1. *Lancashire Memorials of the Rebellion MDCCXV* Samuel Hibbert, 1845 p.37.
2. *The History of The Rebellion in the Year 1715* Robert Patten p.44 & 45.
3. Ibid p.78.
4. *Lancashire Memorials of the Rebellion MDCCXV* Samuel Hibbert, 1845 p.129.
5. *The History of The Rebellion in the Year 1715* Robert Patten p.86.
6. Ibid.
7. Blair Archives 45/12/77.
8. *The History of The Rebellion in the Year 1715* Robert Patten p.88.
9. Ibid.
10. Ibid p.87.
11. Blair Archives 45/12/77.
12. TNA SP54/9/107.
13. *Newcastle Courant* 8 February 1716.

Chapter 13

1. TNA SP54/9/101B.
2. TNA SP54/10/31.
3. History of Clan Gregor from public records and private collections; compiled at the request of the Clan Gregor Society by MacGregor, Amelia Georgiana Murray; Clan Gregor Society Vol II p.290.
4. *The Correspondence of the Rev. Robert Wodrow* Vol 2 Thomas M'Crie (ed.) p.113.& p.114.
5. Ibid.
6. *Memoirs of the Insurrection in Scotland in 1715* John, Master of Sinclair p.192.
7. Ibid.
8. Ibid p.287.
9. *Crucible of the Jacobites* Johnathan Oates p.64.
10. *The Pictorial History of England: Volume 4* George Lillie Craik, Charles MacFarlane p.318.
11. *Memoirs of the Insurrection in Scotland in 1715* John, Master of Sinclair p.217.
12. *The History of The Rebellion in the Year 1715* Robert Patten p.159.
13. *A Fragment of a Memoir of Field Marshall James Keith* p.19.
14. *Crucible of the Jacobite '15* Jonathan Oates p.183.
15. TNA SP54/10/74B.
16. TNA SP54/10/64.
17. *The History of the Rebellion Rais'd Against his Majesty King George* Peter Rae p.311.
18. TNA SP 54/10/45A.

19. *Crucible of the Jacobite '15* Jonathan Oates p.186.
20. NRS GD241/380/22.

Chapter 14

1. Chronicles of Atholl and Tullibardine Families Vol II p.212.
2. Historical Notes; or, Essays on '15 and '45 D. Murray p.84.
3. Chronicles of Atholl and Tullibardine Families Vol II p.213.
4. Ibid p.214.
5. Ibid Addenda cv.
6. Ibid p.213.
7. *Jacobite Prisoners of the 1715 Rebellion* Margaret Sankey p.44.
8. *Lancashire Memorials of the Rebellion MDCCXV* Samuel Hibbert, 1845 p.178.
9. Ibid.
10. *Lancashire Memorials of the Rebellion MDCCXV* Samuel Hibbert 1845, p.176.
11. Ibid p.177 A Letter from a Gentleman in Preston to his friend in the King's Camp Perth.
12. Ibid p.179.
13. Blair Archives 45/12/92.
14. Chronicles of Atholl and Tullibardine Families Vol II p.216.
15. NRAS332/C3/1611.
16. Ibid.
17. Ibid.
18. Blair Archives 45/12/94.
19. Ibid 45/12/95.
20. 6th Report of the Royal Commission on Historical Manuscripts p.702.
21. 6th Report of the Royal Commission on Historical Manuscripts p.702 & 703.
22. Chester and North Wales Architectural, Archaeological and Historic Society Vol 21.

Chapter 15

1. *Diary of Mary Countess Cowper, Lady of the Bedchamber to the Princess of Wales, 1714–1720* p.109.
2. *The History of The Rebellion in the Year 1715* Robert Patten p.182.
3. The Annals of Auchterarder and Memorials of Strathearn p.129.
4. Ibid p.131.
5. The Correspondence of the Rev. Robert Wodrow Vol 3 p.137.
6. Ibid p.153.
7. Ibid p.154.
8. The Annals of Auchterarder and Memorials of Strathearn p.106.
9. TNA SP 54/12/21.

10. *1715: The Great Jacobite rebellion* Daniel Szechi p.167.
11. *Marlborough: The Hero of Blenheim* John Hussey p.126.
12. Jacobite Correspondence of the Atholl family p.6.
13. TNA SP54/11/81.
14. TNA SP54/10/1.
15. TNA SP/55/5/106.
16. Blair Archives 45/12/135.
17. TNA SP54/8/19.
18. TNA SP54/10/99.
19. Blair Archives 45/12/124.
20. Ibid 45/13/162.

Chapter 16
1. The Diary of Henry Prescott LL.B., Deputy Registrar of Chester Diocese Vol II p.483.
2. Ibid p.489.
3. *Jacobite Prisoners of the 1715 Rebellion* Margaret Sankey.
4. Chronicles of Atholl and Tullibardine Families Vol II p.229.
5. The Diary of Henry Prescott LL.B., Deputy Registrar of Chester Diocese Vol II p.491.
6. Blair Archives 45/12/159.
7. Ibid 45/13/47.
8. Ibid 45/13/89.
9. *John Cassell's Illustrated History of England* Vol 4.
10. The Diary of Henry Prescott LL.B., Deputy Registrar of Chester Diocese Vol II p.569.
11. Chronicles of Atholl and Tullibardine Families Vol II p.260.
12. Ibid.
13. Ibid p.262.
14. Ibid.
15. The Diary of Henry Prescott LL.B., Deputy Registrar of Chester Diocese Vol II p.570.
16. Chronicles of Atholl and Tullibardine Families Vol II p.264.
17. Blair Archives 45/13/98.
18. Ibid 45/13/107.
19. Chronicles of Atholl and Tullibardine Families Vol II p.271.
20. Blair Archives 45/13/147.
21. Ibid.
22. Ibid 45/13/164.
23. Ibid 45/14/11.
24. Ibid 45/14/17.
25. *A History of the Western Division of the County of Sussex* Vol 2 James Dallaway.
26. Blair Archives 45/14/67.

27. Chronicles of Atholl and Tullibardine Families Vol II p.321.
28. Ibid.

Chapter 17
1. Chronicles of Atholl and Tullibardine Families Vol II p. 237.
2. Ibid p.228.
3. *Jacobite prisoners of the 1715 Rebellion* Margaret Sankey p. 32.
4. Chronicles of Atholl and Tullibardine Families Vol II p.251.
5. Ibid p.250.
6. Ibid p.245.
7. Ibid p.256.
8. Blair Archives 45/13/89.
9. Blair Archives 45/13/109.
10. Chronicles of Atholl and Tullibardine Families Vol II p.257.
11. Ibid p.305.
12. Ibid p.317.
13. Ibid p.341 ADDENDA cxliv.
14. Ibid p.359.
15. *Lord George Murray and the Forty-Five* Winifred Duke p.36.
16. Blair Archives Jac.C.1. (2) 14 & 15.
17. Chronicles of Atholl and Tullibardine Families Vol II p.356.
18. Ibid p.361.
19. Chronicles of Atholl and Tullibardine Families Vol II p.369.
20. *Caledonian Mercury* 3 December 1724.
21. Chronicles of Atholl and Tullibardine Families Vol II p.369.
22. Ibid p.379.
23. Ibid p.445.
24. Ibid p.371.
25. Ibid Addenda clviii.
26. Ibid Addenda clxv.
27. Ibid Vol III p.19.

Epilogue
1. Chronicles of the Atholl and Tullibardine Families Vol III p.19.

Bibliography

Blair Archives
Hamilton Archives
National Records of Scotland
National Register of Archives for Scotland
The National Archives
British Newspapers Archive
A.K. Bell Library, Perth

Atholl, 7th Duke of John, (collected and arranged by) *Chronicles of the Atholl and Tullibardine Families Vol 1 – 111* (Privately printed at the Ballantyne Press 1908)

6th Report of the Royal Commission on Historical Manuscripts Part 1 (Eyre and Spottiswoode, 1877)

Addy, J & McNiven, P., (eds) *The Diary of Henry Prescott, LL.B., Deputy Registrar of Chester Diocese Vol 2* (Alan Sutton Publishing Ltd, 1994)

Anderson, Rev. James, *The Ladies of the Covenant. Memoirs of Distinguished Female Characters, embracing the period of the Covenant and the Persecution* (Blackie & Son, 1862)

Aufrere, A., (ed.) *The Lockhart Papers Vol I & II* (Richard and Arthur Taylor, 1817)

Baynes, John, *The Jacobite rising of 1715* (Cassell, 1970)

Brown, Peter, (ed.) *Early Travellers in Scotland* (David Douglas, 1891)

Constable, Thomas, (ed.) *A Fragment of a Memoir of Field Marshal James Keith Written by Himself 1714–1731* (The Spalding Club, 1843)

Cowmeadow, Dr Nicola, *Simply a Jacobite Woman? The Life Experience of Lady Nairne* https://media.nationalarchives.gov.uk/index.php/simply-jacobite-woman-life-experience-lady-nairne 17 August 2016

Cowmeadow, Dr Nicola, *Scottish Noblewomen in the era of the Union of 1707 – The Religious Writing of Katherine, first Duchess of Atholl'* (Journal of Scottish Historical Studies, May 2014)

Cowmeadow, Dr Nicola, '*Your Politick, self designing sister': The role of Katherine, first Duchess of Atholl in the Scottish parliamentary elections of 1702* www.tandfonline.com 20 April 2013

Diary of Mary Countess Cowper, Lady of the Bedchamber to the Princess of Wales 1714–1720 (J. Murray 1864)

Duke, Winifred, *Lord George Murray and the Forty Five* (Aberdeen Milne and Hutchison, 1927)

Fraser, Sarah, *The Last Highlander* (Harper Press 2012)

Graham, E.M., '*Margaret Nairne: A Bundle of Jacobite Letters*' (Scottish Historical Review, 1907)

Graham, E.M., *The Oliphants of Gask Records of a Jacobite Family* (James Nisbet & Co., 1910)

Hibbert Ware, Samuel, *Lancashire Memorials of the Rebellion MDCCXV* (Chetham Society 1845)

Hooke, Nathaniel, *The Secret History of Colonel Hooke's Negotiations in Scotland in favour of the Pretender 1707* (T .Becket, 1760)

Hussey, John, *Marlborough: The Hero of Blenheim* (Orion, 2004)

Kington Oliphant, T.L,. *The Jacobite Lairds of Gask* (Charles Griffin & Co, 1870)

Lee, Sidney, (ed.) *Dictionary of National Biography Vol XXXIX* (London: Smith, Elder & Co. 1894)

Leneman, Leah, *Living in Atholl, A Social History of the Estates 1685–1785* (Edinburgh University Press 1986)

Lenman, Bruce, *The Jacobite Clans of the Great Glen 1650–1784* (Methuen London Ltd., 1984)

Lovat, Lord Simon Fraser, *Memoirs of the Life of Simon Lord Lovat written by himself* (George Nicol, 1797)

Marshall, Rosalind K., *The Days of Duchess Anne* (William Collins Sons & Co. Ltd, 1973)

MacCormick, J., (ed.) *State-Papers and Letters Addressed to William Carstares* (Edinburgh J. Balfour, 1774)

Macky, John, *Memoirs of the Secret Services of John Macky Esq During the Reigns of King William, Queen Anne, and King George I.* (London 1733)

MacKenzie, W.C., *Simon Fraser, Lord Lovat His Life and Times* (Chapman and Hall Ltd, 1908)

MacQuoid, G.S., (ed.) *Jacobite Songs and Ballads (Selected)* (Walter Scott. 1887)

McLynn, Frank, *The Jacobites* (Routledge & Kegan Paul, 1985)

Mitchison, Rosalind, *Lordship to Patronage Scotland 1603–1715* (Edinburgh University Press, 1983)

Oates, Jonathan D., *The Jacobite Campaigns: The British State At War* (Pickering & Chatto, 2011)

Oates, Johnathan, *Crucible of the Jacobite '15* (Helion & Company Limited, 2017)

Paton, Henry, *Papers About the Rebellions of 1715 and 1745 Edited from the Original Manuscripts with Introduction and Notes* (Edinburgh University Press for the Scottish History Scoiety, 1893)

Patten, Robert, *The History of the Rebellion In the Year 1715* Third Edition (James Roberts, 1745)

Petrie, Sir Charles, *The Jacobite Movement* (Eyre and Spottiswoode, 1932)

Rae, Peter, *The History of the Rebellion, Rais'd Against His Majesty King George I By the Friends of the Popish Pretender* 2nd ed. (A. Millar, 1746)

Reid, Alexander George, *The Annals of Auchterarder and Memorials of Strathearn* (David Philips, 1899)

Reid, Stuart, *Sheriffmuir 1715: The Jacobite War in Scotland* (Frontline Books, 2014)

Riley, P.W. J., *King William and the Scottish Politicians* (John Donald Publishers Ltd 1979)

Rose, D. Murray, *Historical notes, or, Essays on the '15 and '45* (William Brown, 1897)

Rose, The Right Honourable Sir George Henry, *A Selection from the Papers of the Earl of Marchmont, On the Possession of The Right Honourable Sir George Henry Rose Illustrative of Events from 1685 to 1750* (John Murray, 1831)

Sankey, Margaret, *Jacobite Prisoners of the 1715 Rebellion* (Ashgate, 2005)

Scott, Walter, *Collection of Scarce and Valuable Tracts on the most Interest and Entertaining Subjects: But Chiefly such as relate to the History and Constitution of these Kingdoms* (T. Caddell and W. Davies, 1814)

Sinclair, John Master of, Memoirs of the Insurrection In Scotland (Abbotsford Club, 1858)

Sinclair-Stevenson, Christopher, *Inglorious Rebellion The Jacobite Risings of 1708, 1715 and 1719* (Granada Publishing Ltd., 1973)

Smart, Edward, *The History of Perth Academy* (Milne, Tannahill & Methven, 1932)

Smout, T.C., *A History of the Scottish People 1560–1830* (Fontana Press, 1972)

Stater, Victor, *Duke Hamilton is Dead!* (Hill and Wang, 1999)

Szechi, Daniel, *George Lockhart of Carnwarth 1689–1727* (Tuckwell Press, 2002)

Szechi, Daniel, *1715 The Great Jacobite Rebellion* (Yale University Press, 2006)

Taylor, A. & H., *1715: The Story of the Rising* (Thomas Nelson and Sons Ltd, 1936)

Tomasson, Katherine, *The Jacobite General* (William Blackwood & Sons, 1958)

Von Den Steinen, Karl, *In Search of the Antecedents of Women's Political Activism in Early Eighteenth-century Scotland: the Daughters of Anne, Duchess of Hamilton*, in Women in Scotland c.1100–c.1750 edited Elizabeth Ewan and Maureen M. Meikle (Tuckwell Press, 1999)

Wodrow, Rev. Robert, *The Correspondence of the Rev. Robert Wodrow Vol III* (The Wodrow Society, 1843)

Index